sock it to me

16 PROJECTS SEWN FROM SOCKS
CREEPY, CRAZY & STRANGELY APPEALING

Brenna Maloney

stash

an imprint of C&T Publ.

Text, Photography, and Artwork copyright © 2012 by Brenna Maloney

Publisher: Amy Marson

Creative Director: Gailen Runge

Art Director / Cover Designer: Kristy Zacharias

Editor: Cynthia Bix

Technical Editor: Teresa Stroin

Book Designer: Kristen Yenche

Production Coordinator: Jessica Jenkins

Production Editor: Alice Mace Nakanishi

Illustrator: Brenna Maloney

Photography by Chuck Kennedy

Published by Stash Books, an imprint of C&T Publishing, Inc., P.O. Box 1456, Lafayette, CA 94549

Library of Congress Cataloging-in-Publication Data

Maloney, Brenna.

Sock it to me : 16 projects sewn from socks - creepy, crazy & strangely appealing / Brenna Maloney.

pages cm

ISBN 978-1-60705-645-4 (soft cover)

1. Soft toy making. 2. Socks. I. Title.

TT174.3.M3618 2012

646.4'2--dc23

2011051166

Printed in China

10 9 8 7 6 5 4 3 2

◇◇◇◇◇◇◇◇◇◇◇◇◇◇◇◇◇◇◇◇◇◇◇◇◇◇◇◇◇◇◇◇◇

Acknowledgments

This book is dedicated to my readers. Thanks to all who've reached out and shared their stories and their own creations with me. It's been a real privilege. This book is also dedicated to George Clooney. Although he has yet to pay my mortgage or actually meet me, I'm sure we are soul mates, and he would not use the word "stalker" to describe me.

I want to thank my great team at C&T Publishing once again. How they put up with me, I'll never know. Special thanks go especially to C&T publisher Amy Marson for giving me my start. Thanks to Susanne Woods for that very first phone call years ago (I told you I burned dinner, didn't I?) and, of course, to my fantastic editor, Cynthia Bix. Without Bix, well, really, what's the point?

And how would I do this without my family? I'm so grateful for my husband's incredible patience and great gifts as a photographer. He *could have* had me committed after I tried to set my sock devil on fire. (Hey, I thought it would make a neat special effect for the book!) But no, he got out the fire extinguisher and all was forgiven.

My parents and sister never seem to think I'm too weird. I always feel their support and love.

And then there are my sons. They're everything, you know. Everything.

contents

sockin' it to ya

a little philosophy

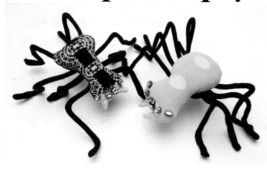

Okay. The gloves are off. This will be the third book I've written for you. I've played it safe. I've made you sweet wittle bunnies and cutie-pie monkeys. It's all been rainbows and unicorns. Until now. Now it is time for The Dark Side of Sock Creatures (cue scary music).

This book completes the sock book trilogy (oh, you didn't know we were doing a trilogy?). Where my first book, *Socks Appeal*, introduced you to the world of sock creatures, and my second, *Sockology*, offered advanced techniques for making sock creatures,

Sock It To Me reveals the dark and seedy side of sock creatures. If you didn't realize socks could be dark and seedy, then you obviously have never done my sons' laundry.

I hope you have a strong constitution. This book is not for the faint of heart. Here we'll be welcoming sixteen horrible new sock patterns, from bedbugs to blood-sucking bats to snowman assassins. You look like a sturdy soul. You can probably handle evil clowns and poison mushrooms. Of course, if rendering the devil out of a sock is too much for you, well, then, maybe this book isn't for you after all. Just give it to your sister and move on.

Let me be up-front about all of this. Clowns give me nightmares. Sloths make my skin crawl. I can't even talk about grasshoppers. This book is full of loath-some things. Now why on earth would I give you a book of loathsome things? Who would want to make these things? Fair question.

First of all, in my defense, the patterns picked me; I didn't pick them. I never pick them. They come to me in the shower, in the car, in my sleep. They never come politely. They come rattling into my brain at Warp Factor Nine and there isn't a darn thing I can do about it. They are relentless. They are demanding. They pester me and whine and cause all sorts of irritation until I just sit down and make one. Or six.

Second of all, just because the thought of a grasshopper makes me want to gouge my eyes out with a hot stick doesn't mean they aren't *your* favorite insect. You might wuv them to wittle pieces. To each his own. Who am I to judge? You might want to make a sloth because it's funny. Or because it reminds you of a co-worker. You might want to make a devil as a gift ... maybe to give to a person in your orbit who sucks the very life out of you. Not ... that ... I ... knowanythingaboutthat-whatsoever. You might want to take on the mighty anglerfish because it's a great challenge and because it looks weird and cool. We all have our reasons, don't we?

This book is just a kind of exorcism for me, you know? I'm just *getting the demons out* so I stop hearing the voices. What you do with them, well, that's up to you.

tool belt

You're a seasoned pro. I can tell that by the look of you. You've been around the sewing machine a time or two. It's clear you know how to handle yourself. I know that a pro like you has a set of go-to tools. You just never know when you're going to need scissors or a poker, so it's good to always be prepared.

I'm guessing you and I think alike on this front. Except when I picture you, I think of you wearing a gunslinger's belt. I picture you with a full arsenal at your disposal, ready for a quick draw. It's high noon, and something out there needs fixing. Glue gun at the ready!

What do you have in that gun belt, anyway? Scissors, sure. The Big Pair and the Small Pair, because we all have those, right? The mini glue gun. The ol' seam ripper. Don't pretend you don't have one (or that you never need to use one). I know you've got one, and I know it's tucked in that belt. I use mine *constantly*.

Marking pens   Let's talk about these for a second. There are those disappearing-ink types that quilters use. But let me suggest two others for working on socks. When you're tracing around a pattern onto your sock, you don't want anything to bleed through. Try using one of those really fine-tip pens, like Pigma Micron pens. I haven't had any bleed-through problems with them. I'll tell you what else works: white or silver gel pens. Yeah. Especially if you are working with dark socks. I'm pretty sure writing on socks is not these pens' intended use, but that's okay. The gel smears off pretty easily, actually, but not before you've marked and sewn your pattern.

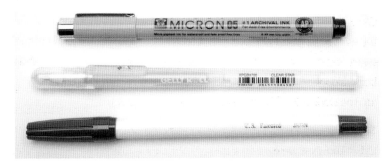

Pokers I'm sure you've got an assortment of pokers for turning sewn sock pieces. Me, I have a favorite kebab stick and a favorite unsharpened pencil. God help me if they ever snap, because I've used them forever. Alex Anderson's 4-in-1 Essential Sewing Tool (available from C&T Publishing) is a fine tool to have in your belt as well.

But let me tell you about something else. This came to me from a reader in Ohio. She sympathized with my earlier whining about how hard it is to turn some of my sock projects. She told me I needed a scissors-like fisherman's clamp (she suggested a Dr. Slick Co. Spring Creek Clamp). Get the five-incher, for fly-fishing. Works brilliantly.

Come to find out, it's the same dang thing my own mother had already given me—a hemostat from a medical supply company. Doctors and nurses use it to clamp off bleeders during surgery. My mother told me she also used it for turning. Well, I forgot all about it and put it in a drawer. Which just goes to show you what happens when you don't listen to your mother. Or *my* mother, for that matter.

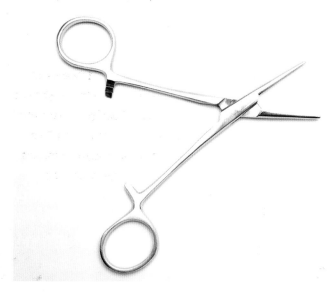

This little baby will change your life; I am not kidding you. It will make you stop your swearing *and* tie off any bleeders, should something untoward happen in your sewing lair. The hemostat or the clamp will help you turn even the tightest, narrowest sock limb/tail/neck by pulling it from the outside (as opposed to your more traditional poker, which you employ from the inside). Thanks to this reader (and my mother, who is always right), turning could not be easier.

With your gun belt all set now, let's move on to supplies. What do we need?

supplies, including "the wig"

In order to make your new sock creations completely "socktastic"—a new word that seems to be sweeping my household, thanks to my older son—you may need to have some of the following supplies on hand.

Thread   You might notice in the photos that I use a lot of contrasting thread when I sew. I'm not colorblind; there's a method to my madness. I want you to see what I'm doing as I do it, so that's what's up with the funky thread. But I don't want you to follow suit. In most cases, you'll want to use a matching thread so your stitches don't show.

Embroidery floss   I go through the stuff at an alarming rate. It's very handy for detail work on faces. In fact, you should always have some on you in case of an embroidery emergency. Don't leave home without it.

Felt   You'll need sheets and sheets of it! Well, okay, maybe not that much. But if you have a good array of colors, I think you'll be turning to your stash for making mouths and eyes when you make these projects.

3805

Pipe cleaners I probably use too many. They're just incredibly useful if you want to put some scaffolding in your creatures. I like to do this to help give them more character and life. If you prefer your stuffed animals to be floppy, then, by all means, just ignore me when I tell you to reach for yet another pipe cleaner.

Paint We'll try paint on a few projects in this book. I'm rather fond of Jacquard's Lumiere acrylic fabric paint, which you can find in craft stores. The colors are iridescent and unbelievable. The paint sticks well to most socks, too.

Buttons, big and small Buttons are always great for eyes. I've discovered that smaller buttons can also be useful for movable limbs. You'll see that these small ones are called for in a couple of the patterns in this book.

Beads and bling   Sometimes, the shiner, the better! I love black seed beads (especially for tiny eyes). Larger beads with weird knobs are also great for unusual eyes. And we'll even use microscopic glass beads during an experiment in this book (see Shifty Chameleons, page 94).

Ribbon   Always good for tails. Ribbon can also sometimes be used for hair, or you can even use it on your Wicked Weeds (page 60) instead of petals.

Tiny pom-poms   Not usually in my arsenal, I have to admit. But these little babies really came in handy for some noses in this book.

Stuffing   Most of these projects will require polyfill stuffing. You can use rice for stuffing, too. (You can also cook it up for a tasty snack, should you get hungry.) In this book, we'll use polyfill, rice, and quilt batting to fluff our stuff. The batting makes a good stuffing for flat things like the Dastardly Devilfish (page 88) or Itchy Bedbugs (page 48).

Clown wig   Okay ... I *might* ask you to acquire a clown wig. Details later ...

And, of course, SOCKS   You'll need a few socks. Well, maybe "a few" doesn't quite cover it. ... It's the usual suspects.

Crew

And, naturally, ANKLETS!

Backstitch

Running stitch

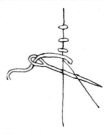

Slip stitch

What is she talking about?

In many places in this book, I'll advise you to hide your stitches when hand sewing. What am I talking about? Use a tiny slip stitch. I don't like my stitches to show, so I'm always careful to hide them.

theme music

Theme music? Did you read that right? Yes, you did. I just wanted to give you a heads-up on this. You may find that some of these sock creatures demand theme songs. You can't really work on Dastardly Devils (page 126), for example, without playing the Squirrel Nut Zippers' "Hell" a few times. Puts you right in the mood. Try it. You'll thank me later. Scott Joplin's "Pine Apple Rag" is awfully good for Shifty Chameleons (page 94), for some reason. Or try this: Find a copy of Khachaturian's "Sabre Dance" when you make an Itchy Bedbug (page 48). So, so fun!

Don't underestimate the power of music. When you're in your lair late at night and you're feeling a little foolish because you're sewing your seventeenth Wicked Weed—and what kind of nonsense is that, anyway?—you might need a little musical comfort.

I also use music when I get stuck. On one of these patterns I think I must've listened to John Mellencamp's "Rumbleseat" 86 times because I just couldn't get the pattern sorted out and I felt like a loser.

If you just need to clear your head before setting to work, then find a copy of Sir James Galway playing Vivaldi's The Four Seasons. Listen to "Winter." Listen and weep, my friends. The purity of those notes. Man alive. He is a master. You listen to that and you will be able to do anything.

◇ **Rules to Live By** ◇

Before you dive in, remember these simple rules.

- If a project calls for one of the patterns in this book, photocopy it (they're full size), cut it out, and use a marking pen to trace around it onto your sock.

- You can sew by hand if you like. I use my trusty Kenmore sewing machine.

- Turn socks inside out when you cut and stitch the body parts together.

- Try to maintain a ¼" (0.5 cm) seam allowance on most of these projects, if possible.

- Always leave a gap of ½"–1" (1.25 cm to 2.5 cm) when you stitch the body so you can turn it right side out before stuffing.

- Stuff fully, but don't pack too tight (unless I tell you to).

- Use a slip stitch to close up the gap after stuffing.

- To hand stitch limbs and other parts to your beasties' bodies, fold under the raw edges and use a slip stitch.

And always follow your dream! Unless it's the one where you're at work in your underwear during a fire drill. Don't. Do. That.

suckitude/ sockitude

You know my theory on this. We've talked about it before, haven't we? Imperfection is okay. Sometimes, it's actually preferred! You fail only if you quit. Everything else is considered a win. That's not to say that you can't put a project down for a bit if things aren't going your way. Geez, I once got so frustrated, I locked a pattern up in a drawer. Mostly because I was afraid it might find its way out and attack me. The point is, any time you create something, you're putting yourself out there. You're going to have moments when you're one with the universe and what you make is *the best thing ever*. And … you're going to have other moments when you find you've sewn an extra limb on something and now you want to scream (see seam ripper, page 5). I get it. I'm with you. You can vent to me. Let it all out. Do you need a tissue? That's better now, isn't it? Let's just sit here quietly for a few minutes before we give it another go, shall we?

things you should be afraid of

Designed and made by Brenna Maloney

snowman assassins

First project in the book, and I'm about to ruin one of your long-held beliefs. Snowmen are *not* nice. There. I said it. You're old enough to come to grips with this kind of truth. Forget all about happy, jolly snowmen—especially in the sock world. Sock snowmen are trained killers. They can pelt you with a 70-mile-an-hour snowball before you can even say, "Please, just take the money."

Snowman Assassins are surprisingly simple to make. All you need are three sock balls. Now when I say "sock balls," I do *not* mean the kind of sock balls that my sons create when they peel their nasty, sweaty socks off their sticky, hot feet. No. The Assassins are made from a different sort of ball, and they come in three sizes. I'll explain as we go.

1. Find a pair of long knee-highs.

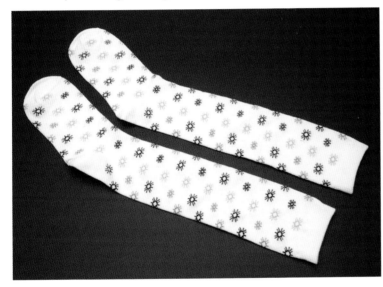

2. We're going to have to get a bit creative cutting these puppies up. Take a look. We're cutting the cuffs off the tops, then cutting the first sock into 3 segments, and the other into 6 segments.

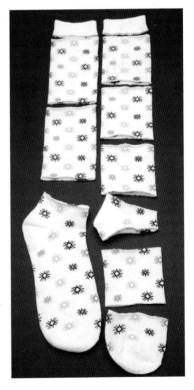

3. Each Assassin is made up of 3 balls—small, medium, and large. Each ball is made up of 8 pieces. (You'll find Snowman Assassins body patterns for these on page 134.) Once you learn how to create one size of ball, you'll have the secret to creating all of them. So we don't both go blind, we'll start off with the largest ball, using the segments from the first sock. Fold each segment in half across the middle and trace the large body pattern on the top layer with a marking pen. When you cut it out, you'll get 4 pieces.

4. Repeat Step 3 with the second segment. Now you have the 8 pieces you need for the large ball.

5. With right sides together, sew the first 2 slices together along one side.

6. Open it. It should look like this.

tip

Although the patterns I've given you are the sizes I use in this book, feel free to get creative with the copier at work and make larger or smaller ones if you like. (Just don't tell your boss I put you up to it.)

7. Add 2 more slices, and you have half the ball.

8. Keep going and you'll soon have 2 halves. It's sort of fun, right?

9. Join the 2 halves, but leave a small opening so you can turn the ball.

10. Go ahead and turn the ball. Ta-da! That was easy, wasn't it? Hardly looks menacing at all. But just you wait …

11. Repeat this simple process 2 more times using the small- and medium-size patterns and the segments you cut from the second knee-high. Sew exactly in the same way and turn. Don't hurry. I'll wait. But in no time at all, you'll have 3 balls of different sizes.

12. Now, a Snowman Assassin has game. He's got moves. So to give your Assassin some flexibility, let's stuff each ball with rice. Using a funnel will help you direct the rice into the ball and not onto the floor.

13. Carefully hand stitch the openings on all 3 balls.

14. Now we need to put our guy together. How you attach the balls is up to you. You can stitch them together by hand or use a hot glue gun—or the magnets, if you've inserted those. I've just loosely stacked mine on top of each other here to show you, because *before* you attach the middle ball to the head ball, you need to consider the arms.

15. Find something to use for arms. There are many things you can use. I do like using twigs. But bent pipe cleaners also work, as do arms fashioned out of craft wire.

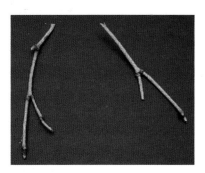

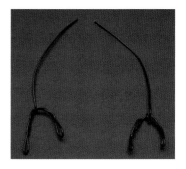

16. Before affixing the snowman's head, add his face. Two eyes made out of coal (or seed beads). Done! How about some evil eyebrows and gritted teeth stitched with a couple of strands of black embroidery floss? Just make simple straight stitches.

17. For his carrot nose, roll an itty-bitty piece of orange felt into a cone. You can stitch this in place using matching thread (or "Hello, Mr. Hot Glue Gun"). Very wicked, indeed.

18. Now you can connect the 3 balls. Whether you are hand stitching or singeing your fingers with the hot glue gun as I so often do, insert the arms between the head and chest balls.

19. Our snowman needs a proper topper, so see the Snowman Assassins hat pattern (page 135) for that. Cut the pieces out of black felt.

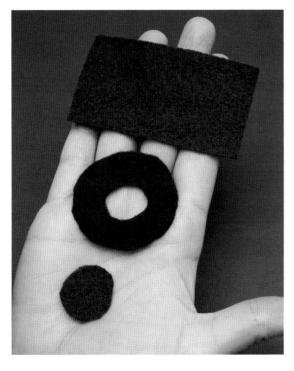

20. Make a tube out of the long piece and hand stitch the ends together.

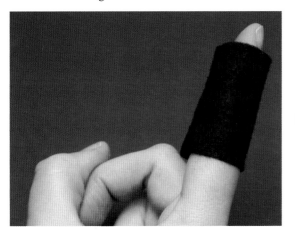

21. Hand stitch the top of the hat to the tube. To attach the brim, it's easiest to use a glue gun.

Voilà! He's looking stylishly disgruntled and ready to pelt you with snowballs.

Violence Can Snowball

Some sock snowmen are sweet ...

... but they quickly fall prey to the bad ones. Here's a nice one trying to say "Hello," while the bad ones yell and make personal remarks.

It's not long before snowball violence breaks out.

It turns out, our nice snowman can give as good as he gets. Take that, Headless!

Designed and made by Brenna Maloney

evil clowns

Finished size: About 6½″ (16.5 cm) tall

When I was describing to a close friend the theme of this book, she kind of snorted and muttered, "Yeah. Clowns." *Clowns?* In contemplating the dark side of things, I have to admit that clowns never really made my list. When I pressed her, she merely said, "Well, everyone knows *they're* evil."

More research was needed. I conducted an informal survey of family, friends, and total strangers, and I'm sad to report that the general consensus is, yes, clowns are evil. Or, at the very least, unnerving. I do hate to malign clowns. I'm sure there are a few out there who are noble and good. Still … the public has spoken. So, I present to you a clown. I tried to make it as evil-looking and disturbed as possible.

1. We'll need 3 anklets to get the job done—a white one, a black one, and a clown one. Well, something that looks clownlike. Think polka dots.

2. Line these suckers up and cut off the heels and toes.

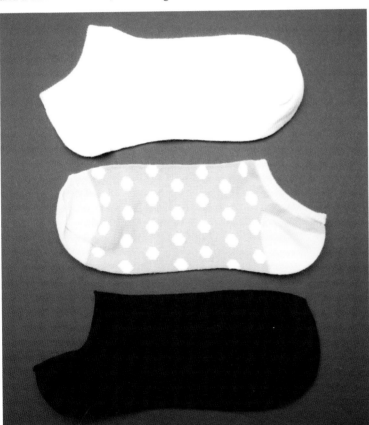

3. Cut open these 3 little tubes so that you have 2 segments of each color.

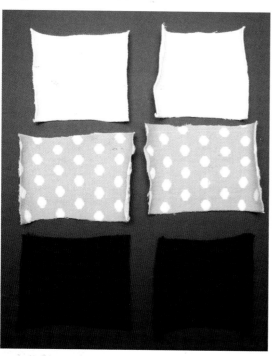

4. Sew together each pair of white and polka dot segments; then sew each white / polka dot segment to a black one. These will be the clown's back and front.

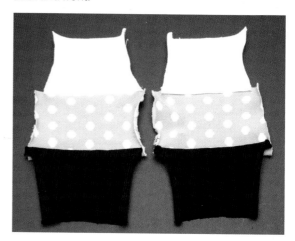

5. Place the front and back right sides together. Photocopy the Evil Clowns pattern (page 136). Yes, I know. Another one of my dreadful hand-drawn patterns. What kind of amateur operation *is* this, you ask? If my pattern is too lame, you can wing it. Just think clown shape—bulbous head, skinny neck, round tum, and little feet. Using my pattern or your own, trace or draw the shape onto the socks with a marking pen. Stitch around the body portion of the shape, making sure to leave a gap in his side for turning. Very important: Hold off sewing his head just yet. You need to add hair first. I got lucky and was able to procure a nasty used clown wig, which I cut into little nasty strands. Or you can use fake fur—orange or red would be terrific. Yarn can also work quite nicely as clown hair.

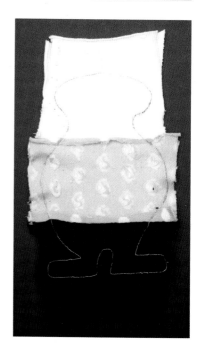

◇ Bad Hair Day ◇

An Evil Clown needs, well, Evil Clown hair. And what is clown hair? I was thinking it was something like Bozo hair—great orange tufts on the side of his head. Probably made out of fake fur? Good instinct, but unfortunately for me, fake fur was not in season when I was coming up with this project. So, I started to panic. What could I possibly use?

Then came Divine Intervention. I happened to be in a thrift store, and there at the bottom of a bin of hats was a rainbow-colored *something*. Could it be? I dug a little further and discovered it was a rainbow-colored CLOWN WIG! My troubles were over! All I had to do was reach in and get the manky thing.

Suddenly, I froze up. Did I really have to … touch it? It was a *used wig*, after all. It had been on some poor clown's sweaty head. And who knows how long it had been sitting in the used hat bin? How badly did I need it? *Badly*, I told myself. *Otherwise, all of your clowns will be bald.*

Sometimes an artist must suffer for her art. I took a deep breath, plunged my hand into the bin, and pulled up the manky used wig. Gingerly pinching it between the tips of two fingers, I all but ran to the checkout counter. For a mere $3.95, the solution to my problem was put into a safe, hygienic plastic bag.

Once home, I cleaned the Evil Clown wig, using multiple cleaning solutions and methods. Then it was ready for me to cut up into little pieces. Which is what you should do, should you be so fortunate as to procure one for yourself. If you have not done so or cannot bring yourself to do so, I understand completely. You may need to wait until fake fur is in season. Or try yarn.

6. Attach your clown's hair. Myself, I snipped choice bits of the wig off (yes, that is me, touching it again), stuck them between the clown head front and back, and stitched that sucker together.

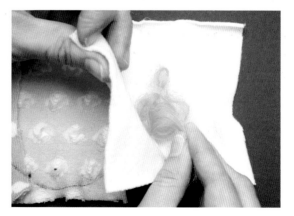

7. After stitching, trim away any excess sock and then turn Evil Clown right side out and have a look. If the hair is all crazy or starts to fall out, it can be course-corrected. Just tame the hair and reposition it, and then seal it in place with a hot glue gun.

8. Lightly stuff His Evilness and sew up the gap we left for turning.

9. Now, to his face. A small, red pom-pom for his nose, if you please. You can try different approaches for the face—felt, embroidery thread, even paint. Just make him look evil and a little demented. He has an image to uphold.

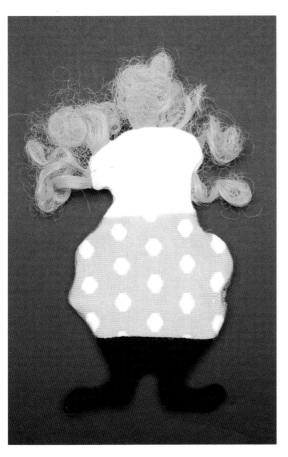

Clown Lineup

For formal occasions, Mr. Evil Clown likes to accessorize with a ruff.

The dunce cap doesn't *really* mean stupid, does it?

Clearly, this one's got "serial killer" written all over him.

Hey! Did somebody remember to bring the whoopee cushions?

Designed and made by Brenna Maloney

sinister anglerfish

I'm very fond of this denizen of the deep. I've looked at photos and marveled at how sinister and lethal it seems. And even the sock version doesn't disappoint. My youngest son calls it Vischy, which is a blend of "vicious" and "fish" (although when he says it, it sounds cute). Anglerfish have a weird little appendage that they dangle over their heads. It has *bioluminescence.* Which means that in the dark of the ocean deep, the end of this thing glows. Other fish see it and mistake it for something yummy to nibble on. As they get close to the angler's "lure," the angler charges and makes quick work of its would-be attacker. Nasty, eh?

1. Let's start with 2 white knee-highs. The color ultimately won't matter because we're actually going to paint this fish.

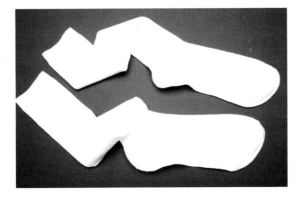

2. Cut off the foot sections of both socks and slice open each sock along the side.

3. Photocopy the patterns for Sinister Anglerfish (page 137). Using a marking pen, trace the body pattern onto the back side of one of your socks. Then, with right sides of the 2 socks together, carefully stitch the outline of the body. You'll be leaving 3 openings—one at the top of the fish's head, one under his belly for turning, and the third at his mouth.

4. Trim away the excess sockage.

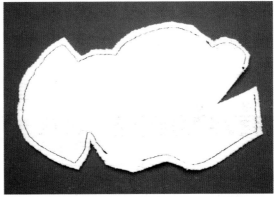

5. Grab one of the foot sections that you cut off earlier. Cut a rectangle about 5″ (12.5 cm) long from the belly of it. Turn under and hem one end. It doesn't matter if your thread doesn't match here because we will be painting over everything later.

6. Here's where things get a bit weird. To make a glowing lure for our sock angler, we'll need a cheap reading light, the kind you can pick up at the dollar store. It doesn't matter what color because we're going to put it inside our fish.

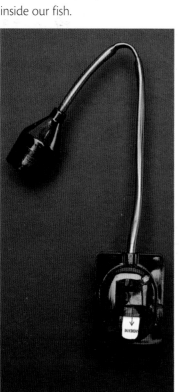

tip

If you can't find a cheap reading light, tightly braid 3 pieces of pipe cleaner together to make a thick "stem." Glue a marble to one end.

7. Take the hemmed rectangle from Step 5, fold it in half, and sew the long edges together to form a tight tube that will fit around the neck of the book light or braided pipe cleaner.

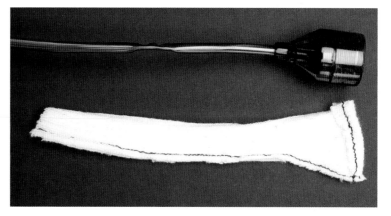

8. Turn the tube right side out and insert the book light or pipe cleaner "lure." You might want to add a touch of hot glue around the edges of the light in order to keep the sleeve from slipping down later. Set it aside for now.

9. On the other foot section you cut off earlier, use the mouth lining pattern (page 137) to cut 2 large squares with rounded edges. It's going to be much larger than we need for the mouth, but it gives us something to work with. (These pieces are not sewn together yet; they are just stacked.)

10. This next step is a bit of a headache, but just go very slowly and it will be okay. It's going to be imperfect, but we want that here. Trust me. Your fish will look really cool. Open the mouth on the fish's body.

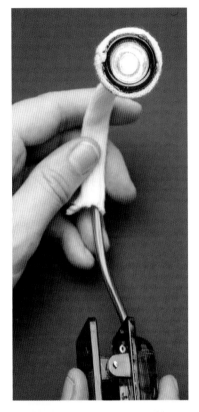

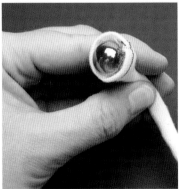

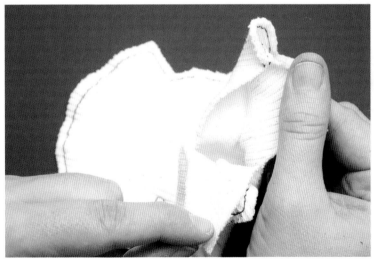

11. Fit the unsewn 2-ply mouth lining inside the mouth. Pin the lining along the edges of the mouth.

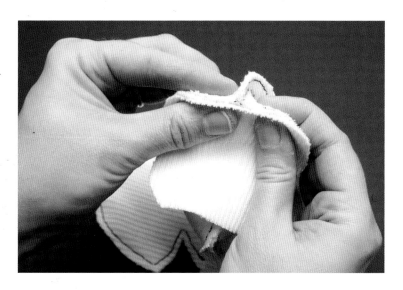

12. Carefully stitch along the contours of the mouth, connecting the mouth lining with the fish's mouth opening. You can see here how much extra sock we have on the mouth piece (left). Here it is from the other side (right). That's all okay. Just trim away all the excess sockage here.

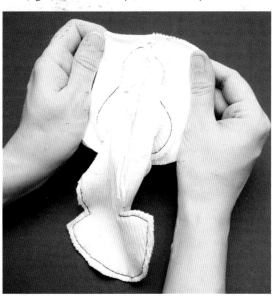
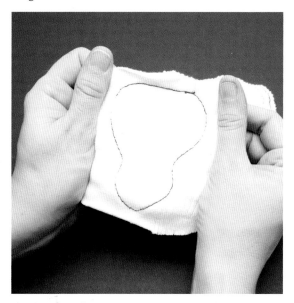

13. Now turn your fish. See how his mouth looks now?

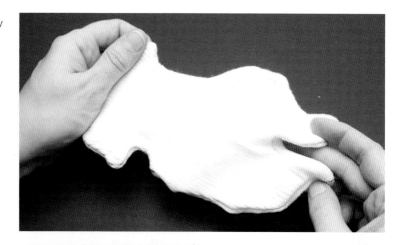

14. Stuff the sock-covered flashlight (or marble and pipe cleaner) into the body of the fish and out through that opening we left in the top of the head/body.

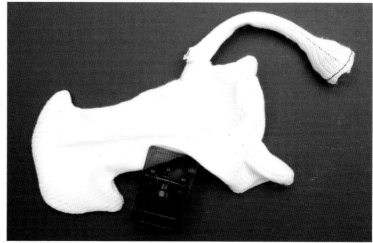

15. Carefully hand stitch the bottom of the flashlight sleeve to the head opening.

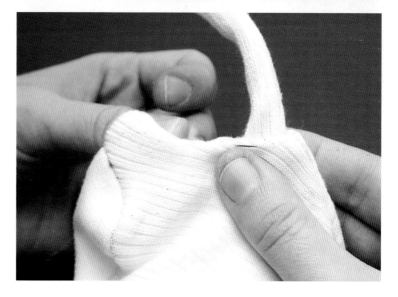

16. Gently stuff the fish with polyfill. Start with the tail. If you're doing the flashlight method, hold it in place in the middle of the fish and stuff around it, making sure the body of the light stays centered. Work slowly. Then hand stitch the gap we left open for stuffing.

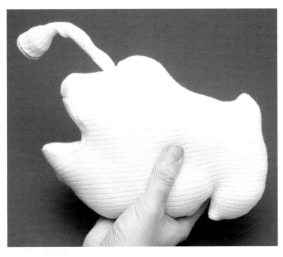

17. With scraps left over from your cut-up socks, use the fin pattern to trace a set of fins for your guy.

18. With 2 layers right sides together, stitch around each fin shape. Trim the excess and turn. I didn't stuff mine, but I did sew long grooves in them just to give them some texture.

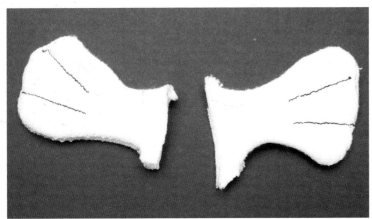

19. Hand sew the fins to your fish.

20. Now we're ready to experiment with paint. I mixed several colors of acrylic paint—a turquoise, a green, and a gold. I just poured a little from each jar into a tray and stirred. There's no right or wrong here. I was going for a certain type of murky green with gold highlights. Your fish can be any color you like. I used Jacquard Lumiere acrylic paint because it's iridescent, which is how I picture the scales looking. I used a foam brush and put the paint on pretty thickly.

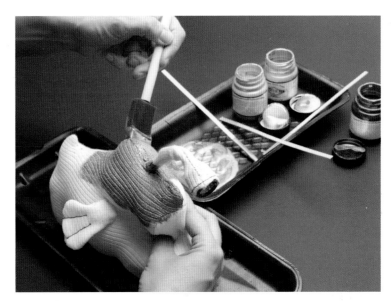

21. Once your fish is all painted, leave him alone for a day or two to dry.

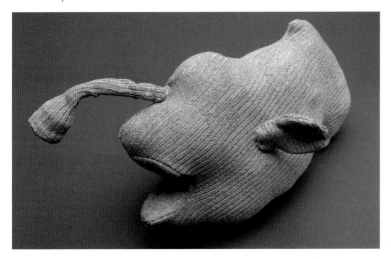

22. When the fish is dry, add some eyes—beads, perhaps. And look for something fantastic for his teeth. Anglerfish have really gruesome teeth. I was lucky to find these jagged shell beads, which I hot glued into place.

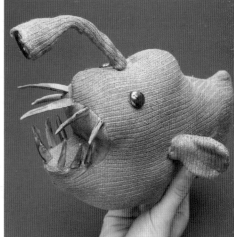

tip

In order to click Anglerfish's light on, you'll need to find the switch from the outside. This can be a little tricky at first, but you'll soon get the hang of turning him on and off. If you find it too frustrating to do it like that, you can always leave that small gap in his belly open and just reach in with your finger to move the switch.

Looking for Lunch

Delicious! Can I have some?

Uh ... guys? Can we talk about this?

things you should avoid

Designed and made by Brenna Maloney

blood-sucking bats

Wingspan about 9″ (23 cm) claw to claw

ats are the only mammals naturally capable of true and sustained flight. They are awe-inspiring. But we fear them because they are butt ugly. Have you ever looked at random bat pictures before? Do it right now. Go to Google and type in "bat"; click on "Images." Some bats have ginormous earlobes. Others have pig snouts. Some have skin that looks entirely too loose for their bodies. They're almost always rabid. And they *all* thirstily suck people's blood with their pointy, pointy fangs. Okay, well, I made up those last two things. But see how easily it happens? If you aren't attractive, people look for reasons not to like you. It's a shallow and cruel world. They're bats. What's to love? Oh, sure, their mothers love them. And you'll love the sock version of them, but let's be honest: For a mammal, people would rather look at hamsters. Doesn't matter to *us*. We're not like that. So, let's add a few bats to our belfry, shall we?

1. Now, your bat can be any color. I chose a pair of long black knee-highs to get us started.

2. A lot of slicing and dicing to be done here. On your first sock, cut off the cuff and the foot. Cut a 2" (5 cm) segment for Bat's ears, a 3" (7.5 cm) segment for the head and gusset, and a 4" (10 cm) segment for the body. On your second sock, just remove the foot and the cuff.

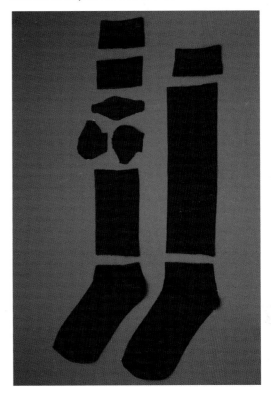

3. Photocopy the Blood-Sucking Bats patterns (page 138). With a marking pen, trace and cut out 2 heads and a middle head part thingy (gusset, for those English speakers out there) from the 3″ (7.5 cm) segment.

> ### tip
>
> Since we are using a black sock, it's going to be murder to mark the pattern and be able to see it. (Well, *I* am using black, at least. *You* might be using a polka-dotted sock.) At times like these, I whip out my trusty white gel pen and mark the pattern with that. I've found that gel pens are pretty slick, and the mark doesn't stay on the sock for very long— just long enough for me to mark something and get it sewn.

4. Turn the 2″ (5 cm) segment inside out and either use the Blood-Sucking Bats ear pattern (page 138) or free sew 2 little teardrop-shaped ears.

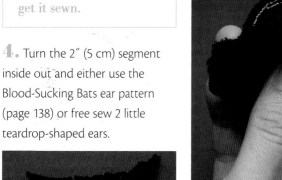

5. Trim away excess sockage and turn the ears.

6. Pin an ear between a side head piece and the gusset. The ear should be facing down. It's a little tricky to line all this up, so feel free to use pins to hold things in place.

7. Stitch across the gusset so the ear is locked in place. Repeat with the other ear and other side of the head. You can turn the head to see how you're doing.

8. Now connect the other side of the head (with the other ear) to the gusset. Stitch from under the chin all the way up to the back of the head.

9. Turn it right side out and take a look at your little bat head.

10. Now let's get to work on Mr. Bat's body. On the 4" (10 cm) segment, mark the pattern, but *do not cut it out.* Sew it first and then cut away the excess. Those bat toes are mighty small. When you're ready, sew slooooowly. Put that machine on "turtle" and do not go over the speed limit. Trim off the excess all around, including around the toes.

11. Turn the body. Remember to use your special tools—see Pokers (page 6)—for turning the toes. By special tools, I'm referring not only to the ones described there, but also to any special breathing or meditation exercises that you like to use during stressful situations. And remember, if nothing works, put it down and walk away. Seek out Junior Mints or the candy of your choice before trying again.

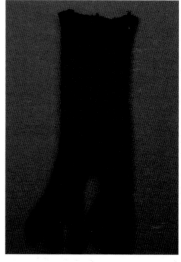

12. Mr. Bat needs his precious toes for hanging upside down, so we'll need to give him some structural support to do that. A trusty black pipe cleaner is just the thing. Bend a small W at one end.

13. Press the loops together to help form the toes, and loop the free end around a couple of times to lock the toes in place.

14. Make a larger loop at the bottom and cut off the excess pipe cleaner. Make 2, one for each foot.

15. Insert the wire feet into the sock feet.

16. Gently stuff the body with polyfill. Not too much. Also stuff the head. Tuck any raw edges under and hand stitch the head to the body using matching thread.

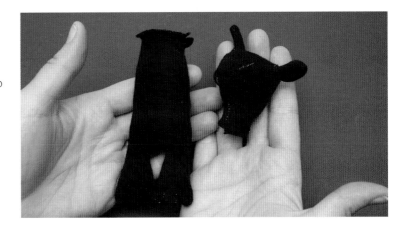

Now Mr. Bat's all in one piece, but he's missing something important. Wings.

17. The fun never ends with this pattern! Go back to the large section you cut from your second sock. Fold it in half with the short ends together.

18. With the fold on the left, free cut (through 4 layers) a pair of wings. They should have a gentle ripple to them.

19. Open the fold, and the wings should look something like this.

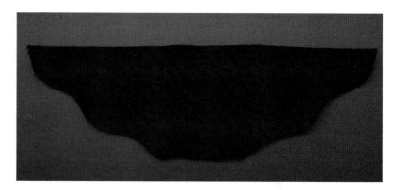

20. Open this piece up and lay a pipe cleaner along the middle. The ends of the pipe cleaner should stretch out beyond the sock. If they don't, twist on another piece to extend the pipe cleaner. You want at least an inch poking out from each end.

21. Close the piece again.

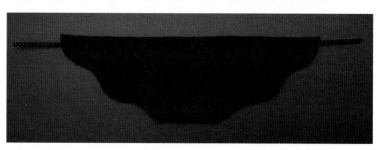

22. Using *black* thread, not crazy turquoise as I've done here, stitch the pipe cleaner in place. Do not sew the ends closed.

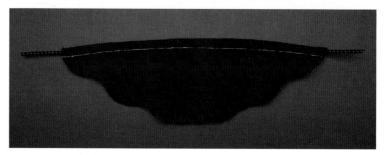

23. We're going to zigzag stitch the edges of the bat's wings, but first, pull out a little sock scrap to test your machine's setting. You want a zigzag stitch that's fairly tight to finish off those edges.

24. Go ahead and zigzag the open edge of the wings, from tip to tip, but do *not* sew the ends by the pipe cleaner closed. I don't mean to shout, but I'm serious about that. You've got a wee bit of pipe cleaner hanging out on both ends, and we're going to need to add to that in a second. Now, you should have a cool rippling effect on the wings.

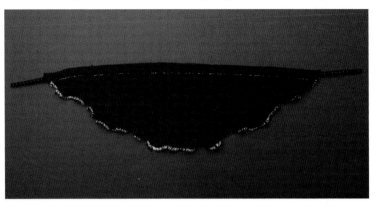

25. Now we're going to use those bits of pipe cleaner sticking out at the ends as part of Mr. Bat's long fingers. Wrap a fresh pipe cleaner around each end just inside the ends of the wings that you left open. Twist several times; you should have 3 prongs. Twist, bend, and trim until you create 3 reasonable-looking "fingers" at each wing tip.

26. Bend the tips of the fingers over to make claws.

Here's the full view of the wings with fingers in place.

27. Hand sew the wings to Mr. Bat's back. Because the wings are 2-ply, you should have no problem hiding your stitches.

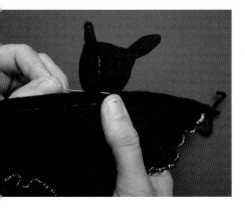

28. Add some beads for eyes.

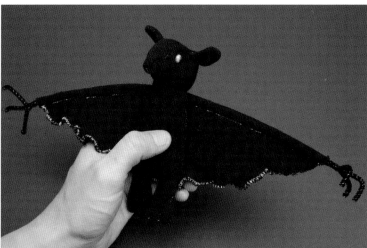

29. Now let's talk about fangs. You have a lot of flexibility here. Felt works. Shaving down craft sticks can work. So does making little white fangs out of Fimo clay. I just happened to have an inordinate number of those little silver clips that sometimes come on new pairs of socks. Why do I save them? I've no idea, but I had quite a pile going, so I wondered if I couldn't just turn a few into fangs. Mr. Bat is looking good.

Now he's ready to hang from trees.

Hanging Out

Does anyone else feel blood draining to their head? Anyone … anyone?

I vant to suck your blood!

Nothing up my sleeve …

Well, I like cashmere wings because they're lightweight but oh so warm in the fall!

Have you guys seen a cricket? About so big?

Designed and made by Brenna Maloney

itchy bedbugs

Finished size: About 4″ (10 cm) long

This is a bedbug. Bedbugs, as you know, are small parasitic animals that lie in wait in your bed so they can nibble on your tender bits while you sleep. If your delicate constitution cannot bear the thought of bedbugs, then I honestly wonder how you came into possession of a book called *Sock It To Me*. But never mind all that. You can think of them as … uh … doodlebugs. Yeah. Sweet wittle doodlebugs. That sounds better, right?

1. Okay, if you've got a grip on yourself now, dig around in your sock pile for a couple of anklets. Look for socks with strong colors. One will be for the body and the other for the mouth and feet. If possible, use a smaller anklet, like a kid's anklet, for these accents. It will just be easier to sew the mouth in if you do. If you don't have anything smaller, an adult-size anklet will work, too.

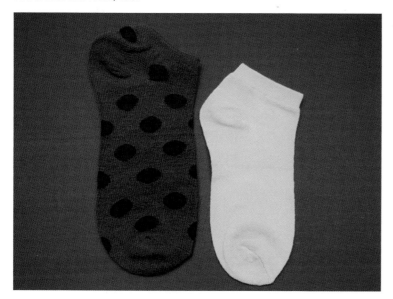

2. Turn your accent sock inside out. For the bug's mouth, cut off the little ribbing part and about ½" (1 cm) of sock with it. On the rest of the sock, free sew 6 little U's. These are going to be your bug's wittle toesies. *Optional:* If you want to add a tongue or fangs, sew 1 or 2 extras.

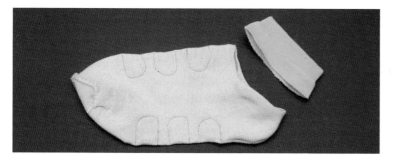

3. Trim and turn the toesies. Now you have 3 for each side, plus the ribbing for your bug's lips. Do bugs have lips? I'm not sure, but I think they do … the better to *suck your blood* with.

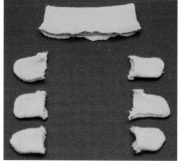

4. On the other sock, cut off the toe, heel, and ribbing sections. The main part of the sock will be the body; round the edges a bit.

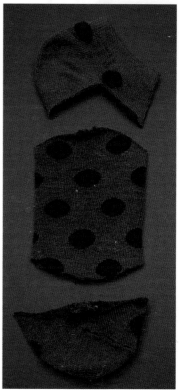

5. Cut 2 pieces of quilt batting to the shape of the body.

6. Now, we'll make a little bug sandwich out of the layers. The recipe is as follows, from bottom layer to top: underbody right side up, 3 legs facing inward on each side, lips (sock ribbing) with folded edge facing inward, top body right side down, both layers of quilt batting. Pin to hold all the layers together.

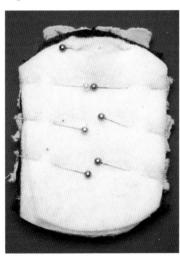

7. Slowly stitch all the way around the perimeter of Bedbug's body, leaving a small gap for turning. Trim away any excess.

8. Gently, gently turn. Then use matching thread to hand stitch the gap you left open.

9. Give the bug some eyes. Now go put this finished bug in your bed—on your loved one's side, of course. See if you get any kind of reaction!

Bugged

Meet Lars and his brother, Olaf. Tough fellas, these. Ol' Lars lost an eye and a leg, but that doesn't stop him from chewing on your leg in the middle of the night.

Ohmygoodness! I should not have eaten that *entire* pillowcase!

If we work together tonight I think we'll be able to bite the entire family!

Designed and made by Brenna Maloney

ssssloths

Finished size: 20"–24" (51 cm–61 cm) long, depending on sock length

he sloth. Of all the animals in our known world, this one skeeves
me out like no other. Is there anything more repulsive? Oh, sure,
it looks kinda cute here, rendered in sock form, but sloths are actually
loathsome and heinous. A sloth moves so slowwwwwwwwwwwwly
that algae actually grows in its fur. Enough said. I can hardly bear to look
at this hideous thing. Why would you want to make such an awful thing?
Well, I don't know. Why did *I* make one? I'm not sure. I'm putting my
money on either temporary insanity or demonic possession. Still. Here
she is, so here we go. . . .

1. Find the longest sock you
can find—a really super-long
thigh-high up-to-the-moon sock.
Cut off the foot section and set it
aside. We'll use that part later for
Sloth's arms.

2. Turn the long section of sock inside out; flatten it so the heel is
facing up and the short open end is at the top.

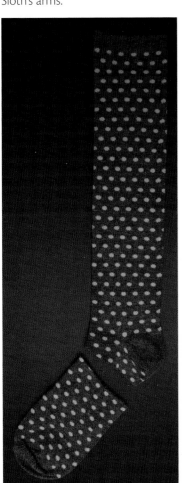

3. Stitch across this opening to form the top of Ms. Sloth's flat little
head. I used contrasting thread for clarity, but you'll want to use
matching thread.

4. At the other end of this piece, free sew 2 long, skinny legs. Leave a small gap for turning, of course, but make the legs as long as you have sock for. The full piece should look something like this, with the head sewn up and the legs formed.

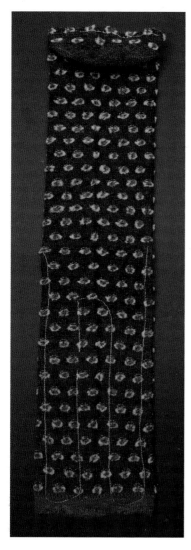

5. Trim away the excess between and around the legs and turn right side out. She looks a little full in the hips here, but we'll even that out as we stuff her.

6. Gently stuff her with polyfill and hand sew that little gap that we left open to turn her.

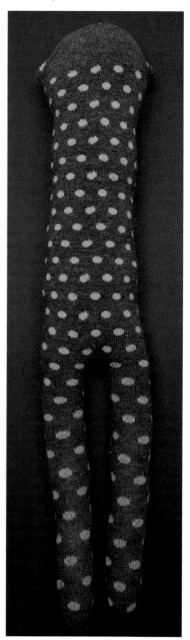

7. Go back to the foot section of the sock and turn it inside out. Sew 2 long arms, using the very tip of the sock's toe for the paws.

8. Trim away the excess and turn. Each hand and arm should look something like this.

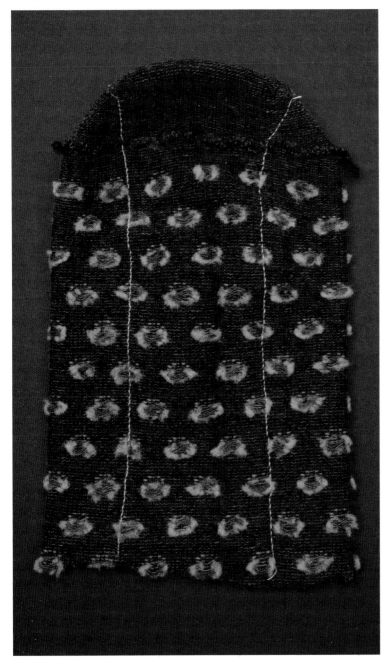

9. As you know, sloths have long, deadly, razor-sharp claws. We've decided this will be a lady sloth, so we're going to give her some bling claws. Diamonds are a girl's best friend, so we'll give her 3 for each paw. (I used long beads.) We'll do the same for the tips of her toes.

tip

You can have fun experimenting with claws. Here are a couple of fine options.

10. Attach her arms to her body, turning the raw edges under as you hand stitch them in place. Try to hide your stitches if you can.

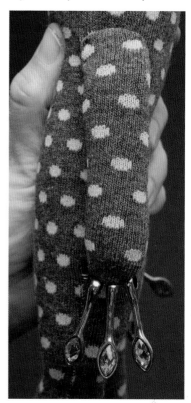

11. For eyes, hand stitch 2 pieces of black felt cut into large ovals, using a matching thread.

12. Now, she really doesn't have any plans for the day. She won't be going "out," for example. Sloths never go anywhere. They eat, sleep, and even give birth hanging upside down from a tree. Still, she'll want to look her best. So, using a backstitch, we'll embroider her a slothful, disgustingly lazy "lipstick" smile using a couple of strands of pink floss.

13. And, if you're really up for it: the finishing touch—false eyelashes!

Lazy Bones

I do nothing all day long, and I like that fine.

So then I said to him, "Well, I can eat that, but it'll take me a full week to digest it. My digestive tract is *that* slow."

Well, I guess *one* of us should move over, but I dunno ... just the thought of it wears me out.

things you shouldn't
touch

Designed and made by Brenna Maloney

wicked weeds

Let's face it: Weeds are thugs. They steal sunlight, food, and water from other plants. They can have nasty prickles and scratchy stems. However, they sometimes disguise themselves by looking beautiful. They can look so beautiful, in fact, that when gardening, your loved one will *swear* they are beautiful flowers. And you can tell said loved one that they are, in truth, heinous weeds that need to be uprooted. *Now.* Then, before you know it, you will get into an argument while brandishing a pair of clippers. You will hear yourself say: *"Look, City Boy. What the heck do you know about gardening? Which one of us is from the Midwest and actually had a yard growing up?"*

Or, well, it *could* happen like that. I wouldn't know, of course. The point is: weeds. No good can come from them.

1. We'll start off with 3 socks—a knee-high and 2 anklets. The knee-high should be some sort of green, as this will be Weed's stem. One of the socks might be yellow, for her face. And the third can be anything you like.

2. Cut the foot portion off the knee-high and turn it inside out. Use the Wicked Weeds leaf pattern (page 139) to mark and stitch 2 leaves—or you can free sew the shapes. These leaves will be Weed's arms. Trim and turn them.

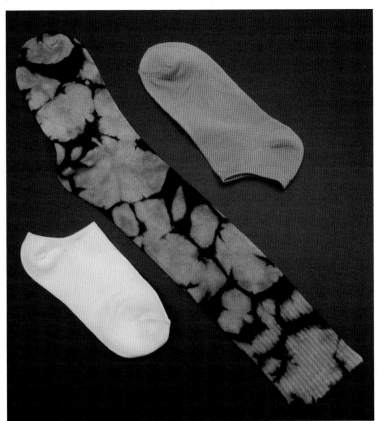

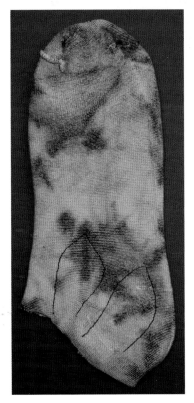

3. Turn the rest of the green sock inside out. We're going to free sew the body. It is long and thin with 2 long, very narrow legs. Trim, leaving about 1½" (4 cm) above the top for the "neck."

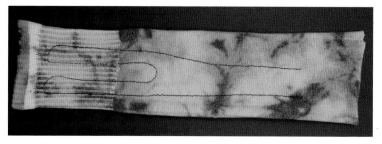

4. Tuck a leaf horizontally inside the neck and pin it.

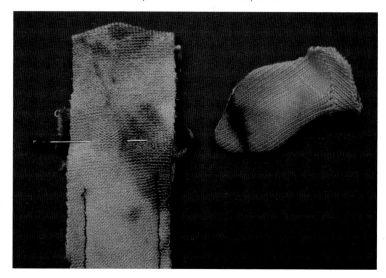

5. Stitch it in place along one side to secure the leaf base; do the same with the other leaf on the other side. You'll have to bunch things up inside to get it all to fit without stitching over the leaf tips. Pinning helps keep things from shifting, but don't be surprised if for the moment Ms. Weed looks like a snake that swallowed an egg. Once you turn her, all will be right with the world again. Set this piece aside.

6. Use the Wicked Weeds face pattern (page 139) to cut 2 circles from your yellow anklet.

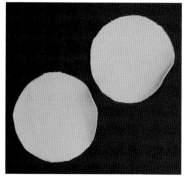

7. Now take your other anklet—the pink one, in my case—and turn it inside out. Use a petal pattern (page 139) to trace and stitch 6 petals. (You'll notice that I gave you a choice of a round or pointy petal.) Or you can free sew 6 petals. I just eyeballed mine, so they look a little crazy, but I think that's okay. She's a *weed*. She's a little crazy to start with.

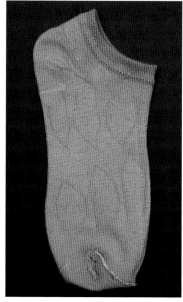

8. Trim away the excess sockage and turn each petal, and you'll see that she's looking more flowerlike by the minute. (Imposter!)

9. Now we're going to position these petals so we can stitch them in place. Pin the little dudes with their pointies facing the center of the yellow circle.

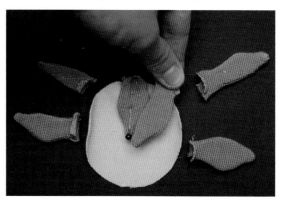

10. Stitch the petals down but—good grief!—don't use black thread like I did. I only did that so you could see what I was up to. And anyway, subtlety was never my strong point. But *you* should use matching thread.

11. Put the other yellow circle on top, facedown.

12. Sew around, but leave a small gap so we can turn Ms. Weed's face.

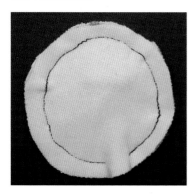

13. Turn her right side out. You'll note that her petals are a little lopsided and her yellow face is anything but perfectly round. Again, I think this is okay because I'm a little lopsided and odd-looking myself. Some of you will undoubtedly have better-looking weed heads, though, and my compliments to you.

14. Now let's get back to the body. Find yourself a couple of pipe cleaners. Twist a little loop on the bottom of each one.

15. Measuring from the bottom up, bend the pipe cleaners in half where Ms. Weed's legs meet her body. Connect the pieces there and then twist the extra pipe cleaner up and out of the way to create a sort of scaffolding for her body.

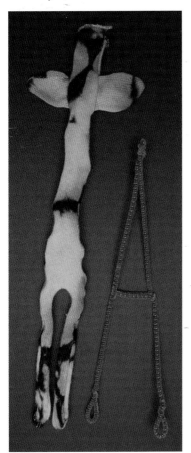

16. Gently push that scaffolding down her open neck hole. Wiggle it slowly all the way down to her feet.

17. Find another pipe cleaner, twist a loop for her head, and wiggle that inside.

18. Add a few pinches of polyfill to stuff her lower tum.

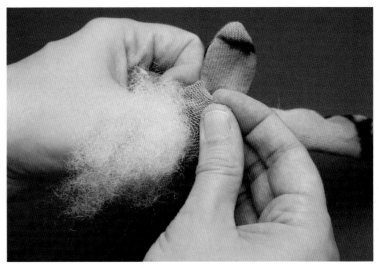

19. Twist the ends of the head pipe cleaner and the body pipe cleaner together to link her top half with her bottom half.

20. Add polyfill in small amounts to her head and the rest of her body. Now you're ready to attach her head to her neck. Be sure to turn the raw edges under and hide your stitches as you hand sew the 2 parts together.

21. Let's give her some eyes. I chose small black pom-poms. Buttons also work well.

22. With a few strands of black embroidery floss, we can use a backstitch to give her a lovely smile. Well, a lovely upside down smile. Ahhh. ... As Keats wrote, "A thing of beauty is a joy forever."

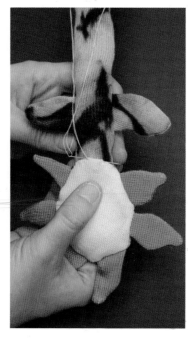

Roundup

Does it seem a little crowded to anybody else in here?

Whose butt can I kick?

Weeds—they are bad. But there's always one black sheep in the family, isn't there? Look at this cheerful fellow, skipping along ... tra la la la.

The other weeds soon make quick work of him. Take that! We'll twist you and your happiness into a pretzel! (I *told* you they were bad.)

Designed and made by Brenna Maloney

killer mushrooms

Finished size: About 4″ (10 cm) tall

ord to the wise: If you are frolicking through the woods one sunny fall day, and you happen to spy some exotic-looking mushrooms, do not—repeat: do not—take them home and eat them. What possesses people to do this? You read about it all the time. In their obits, there's always some neighbor quoted as saying something like, "Well, Dolores was just the nicest gal. I guess she didn't realize she was cooking herself up some Death Cap." Uh, no, I guess not. Not the brightest bulb, our Dolores, now was she? Poison mushrooms always have terrible names, like "The Sickener" or "Destroying Angel." This is a *clue*, people. It means: *Don't eat me. I will kill you, or at the very least give you really serious intestinal distress.* You aren't very likely to nibble on socks, though—Wait, are you?—so the sock version of Killer Mushrooms should be safe in your hands.

1. If you can make a Snowman Assassin (page 14), a poisonous fungus will be no problem for you. We're going to start with a pair of crew socks.

2. You can use any of the Snowman Assassins ball patterns (page 134) to create your mushroom. I'll use the largest one, just so we can see what we are doing. Trace around it with a marking pen.

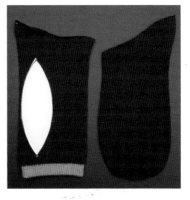

3. You'll need 8 pieces, so lay out your pattern accordingly. You'll need the entire first sock and the toe section of the second sock to get all 8 pieces.

4. Sew the first 2 sections together along one side.

5. Add 2 more sections to make half the ball.

6. Do it again! Do it again! Now you have 2 halves. Do they make a whole? Not yet …

7. … but if you sew them together they will. Remember to leave a small gap when sewing that last segment, because we need to turn the ball.

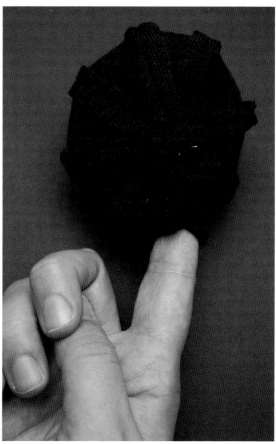

8. Turn that baby right side out! Hand stitch the open end closed with matching thread.

9. Now with your fingers, flatten the ball. If you shape it just so, it should start to resemble a mushroom cap. Not just any mushroom cap, of course. A deadly, poisonous, toxic mushroom cap that is no good to eat!

10. With the remainder of the second sock, free sew a stem. Stems can be about 2½″–3″ (6.5 cm–7.5 cm) tall. They tend to have a bit of a curve to them. The bottom of my stem is going to have that little splash of color from the ribbing on the sock cuff. I like that.

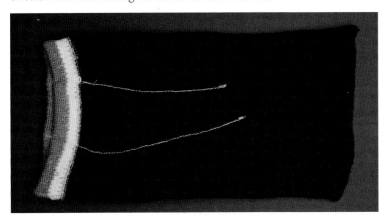

11. Trim the excess sockage and turn.

12. Gather up the end with a running stitch in matching thread and cinch it tight. Mine is bunching up a bit because the sock is rather thick at that end. Make sure it is sealed tightly and knotted well.

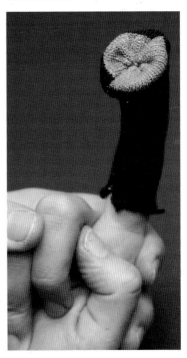

13. In order to give it some flexibility, we'll be stuffing the stem with rice. Whip out your funnel, please, and pour in the rice.

14. Now we have a stuffed stem and a mushroom cap, and doesn't that sound delicious? But you must *resist*! Do not eat!

15. Using matching thread, hand stitch the cap to the stem. Be careful not to let your stitches poke through to the top side of the cap—otherwise, you'll be able to see them on your mushroom's head.

16. With a few strands of embroidery floss in a contrasting color, use a couple of straight stitches to give Mr. Mushroom the perfect expression—sour, but kinda cute. *Bon appétit*, Dolores!

Fungus Among Us

It's dashed uncivilized, Rutherford! The mustache has got to go!

Poisonous? Who, us?

Someday, you'll grow up to be big and toxic like your father, dear.

Feeling ... top ... heavy ... today. Must be Monday. Again.

Designed and made by Brenna Maloney

evil evil bad yucky grasshopper

Finished size: About 4″ (10 cm) long

There is only one of these sock grasshoppers in the entire planet. One, that is, until *you* make one. Me, I'm not going to make any more. I was so traumatized by the making of this one that I'm going to have to retire.

I have a history with these little beasties that, over time, grew into a terrible and cowardly fear of them. Because we are friends, I will tell you the sordid tale. When you're a fifteen-year-old girl growing up in the Midwest and looking for a summer job, you sometimes have to turn to manual labor—for me, it was detasseling corn. I distinctly remember my dad telling me it would "build character," to which I replied, "Don't you and I both think I'm enough of a character by now?" But … off I went to the cornfields.

To detassel corn, you have to walk up and down the rows and yank off the pollen-producing flowers—the tassel—from the tops of corn plants. Not exactly rocket science, but not without its challenges, either. In addition to sweltering heat and razor-sharp leaf edges, the corn also harbored … *things*. Things of an insect nature. Grasshoppers.

As you walked down a row, they would *sproing* past you to get to another row. You've heard the expression "running the gauntlet"? Yeah. It was like that. Take one step. *Sproing.* Grasshopper to the upper chest. Step two. *Sproing, sproing.* Double-whammy assault. Step three. *Sproing, sproing, sproing.* Two to the chest and a direct hit to the face!

So, *sproinging*. And spitting. "Tobacco juice," the farmers called it. Imagine walking down a row of corn, minding your own business, when a grasshopper leaps out of nowhere and sprays you with a mouthful of thick, brown spit. Gotta hand it to them—their aim was good. They rarely missed.

Sproinging, spitting, and *staring*. They had horrid, calculating eyes. They were always watching you, waiting for the moment to strike. I endured three seasons of that.

So, I told my husband that I would make a single sock grasshopper. No other sock grasshoppers exist. And I will not make another. Never. Not ever. No way.

Let's begin.

---

1. You'll need 3 anklets—2 lime green and a yellow.

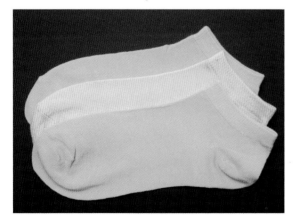

2. The grasshopper, as you surely must know, has an exoskeleton. That means its "bones" are on the outside as a protective shell on its back and underbelly. So, you have to stomp on it pretty hard to

dispatch it. That's *if*—and a big if here—you can get it to hold still long enough to do the stomping. To make his heinous exoskeleton, we're going to cut a rectangle about 3" × 4" (7.5 cm × 10 cm) out of the yellow sock.

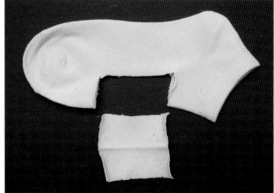

3. Also cut a same-size patch of quilt batting.

4. Place the yellow patch on top of the batting. With green thread, stitch lines across this patch. This will be our you-know-what's underbelly. I used a simple decorative-stitch setting; you can select whatever you like. We're trying to simulate the grooves they have on their underbellies. Notice how tightly I am holding this piece. … I have white knuckles already, and we're only on Step 4.

5. Trim this piece down to a little oval. I've included an Evil Evil Bad Yucky Grasshopper body pattern (page 139) for this, or you can just cut an oval about 3″ (7.5 cm) long. Back it with a piece of muslin cut to the same shape, place them right sides together, stitch, and turn.

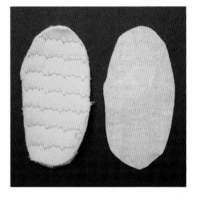

6. Here I had to take a slight break to mop my brow and breathe deeply into a paper bag. Once you are ready to move on, cut a same-size oval out of a green sock and back it with muslin, stitched as in Step 5.

So now you have the foul beast's back and underbelly. Me, I felt a little dizzy here, but I am sure you are just fine.

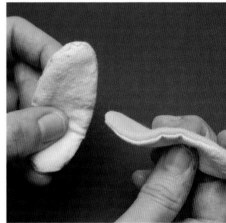

7. Legs. They have 6. The back 2—the longest and most heinous—probably give the sucker the most lift when he pushes off toward you. Turn the other green anklet inside out and free sew 4 short, narrow tubes, about 2½″–3″ (6.5 cm–7.5 cm) long, and 2 longer ones for the back set of legs. You want one end of each of these 2 longer legs to be thicker (think ham hock).

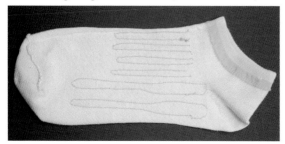

8. Sew the back legs all the way around and then snip a hole in the thigh part to turn.

9. Use that little clampy tool I was telling you about in Pokers (page 6) to turn all the legs. It really will save you on this pattern, because the leg tubes are so very small. I'm not sure, but I may have actually made up a new swear word while I was doing mine.

Here's a look at all the legs, turned.

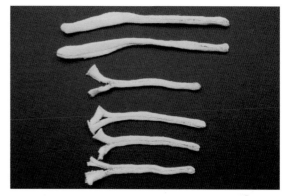

10. Insert little segments of pipe cleaner into the legs. By hand, stitch up the incision you made in the back legs.

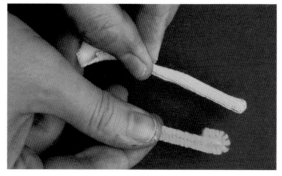

11. We'll need to sew him a nasty little head from the green sock heel. You can check out the Evil Evil Bad Yucky Grasshopper head pattern (page 139) or just wing it. I made mine sort of a triangle, even though grasshoppers' heads are really more elongated. Turn, stuff lightly, and stitch up the gap.

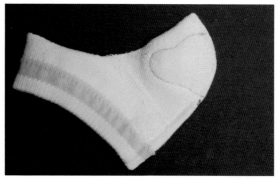

12. Lay the yellow underbelly piece facedown, and put the 4 short legs on top. I used a hot glue gun to glue those suckers down so they wouldn't move while I was sewing.

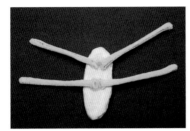

13. Once the glue is dry, lay the green body back piece on top and stitch the whole mess together. Now, I was too nervous to do this, but I'm going to advise *you* to add a little polyfill between the sandwich layers before stitching, to plump up the grasshopper's body a little. Mine looks really flat here. When I finished him, I took a deep breath and went back and added stuffing. You should go ahead and do that now.

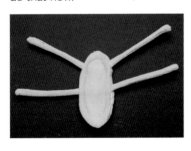

14. With trembling hands, I stitched on his head by hand. You can do it too.

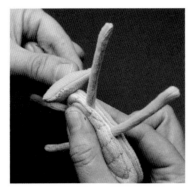

15. You'll need to bend the back legs to make them look right. When you've got that sorted out, hand stitch them to the sides of his body.

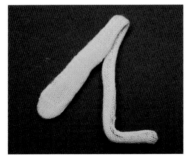

Here he is, all assembled. Yuck!

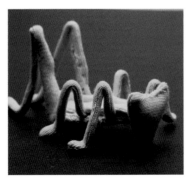

16. Next, give him some nasty little red bead or button eyes. For antennae, poke a small section of green craft wire (about 6″ [15 cm] long) through his head and then curl the ends around a kebab stick.

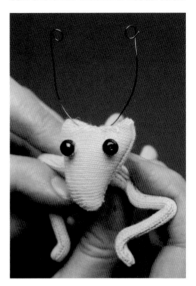

He's done. The consensus in my house is that he looks "cute." I'm going to take a shower now and try never to think about this experience again.

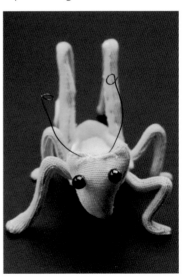

The Green Menace

Crouch ...

Sproinnnnnng!!

Designed and made by Brenna Maloney

not-so-itsy-bitsy spiders

Finished size: About 4½″ (11.5 cm) long

To make this pattern *really* effective, you need to start referring to it as the "spee-EYE-der." It sounds much more exotic that way. So, when you are ready to go make one, you must announce in a loud voice: "I'm going to my lair now to create … (pause here for dramatic effect) … the *spee-EYE-der!*" Then, whirl around and disappear into your lair. A little maniacal laughter might not be a bad idea, either.

1. Now that we're off to an excellent start, find yourself a cool-looking anklet. Something bright and interesting. I chose this Day-Glo argyle. In real life, the colors are nearly blinding. We had to put a special filter on our camera lens to protect your eyes. (I made that up, but it sounds very dramatic and adds to the allure of the spee-EYE-der, don't you think?) Anyhoo, rustle up a good anklet. And while you're rustling, also find yourself a long black knee-high.

2. Cut the foot portion off the black knee-high. Take the long piece that's left and turn it inside out. Sew 4 long, narrow tubes. I'm using a contrasting thread here so you can see what I'm doing, but you should use a matching thread. What we're making are the spee-EYE-der's legs. If you like, you can leave a small opening to turn them. I closed all of mine, though, and you'll see why in a second.

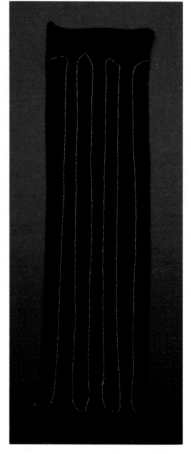

3. Trim around the leg tubes to free them from each other. Then, make a small slit in the middle of each tube.

4. Turn all 4 tubes. If this starts to go badly, use your special turning tools as described in Pokers (page 6).

5. Now we'll need some pipe cleaners. To avoid getting poked later, turn the end of your pipe cleaner down and twist the end around the stalk.

6. Slide the pipe cleaner into the leg tube. If the leg is especially long (or the pipe cleaner is especially short), you may need to use 2 in each leg. If that's the case, don't despair. Well, as a general rule, you should never despair over pipe cleaners. I mean, really, don't you think that's a silly thing to be in despair over? There are other things—my mortgage, for starters. But especially do not despair in this case because all you have to do is twist another one onto the end and keep threading.

7. Once you have all the legs done, hand stitch the leg slits closed with matching thread. You should now have 4 wired and sealed legs. "But wait, Brenna!" you're saying. "I know my anatomy, and spiders (even spee-EYE-ders) *clearly* have 8 legs, not 4." Yes, yes, I know that, too. I'm getting to that. Just keep your shirt on. We have to pause a moment and deal with some body issues.

8. Trace my less-than-fabulous spee-EYE-der body pattern (page 140). Turn your anklet inside out and use the pattern to cut out Ms. Spider's body. I'm getting a nice little triangle pattern going on here because of the anklet I chose.

9. Rustle up a little scrap from your black sock. Turn the piece inside out and free sew 2 pointy, pointy fangs. Make them especially vicious-looking, if you don't mind. Ms. Spider relies on those fangs to subdue her prey and then suck it dry.

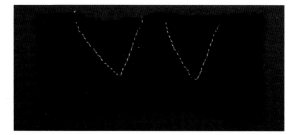

10. Trim the fangs and turn them right side out.

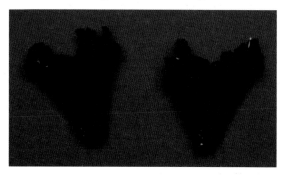

11. Put the 2 body pieces right sides together and sandwich the fangs in between on the top of the head. Pin in place.

12. Sew almost all the way around the body, locking the fangs in place. Leave a small opening so you can turn Ms. Spider right side out.

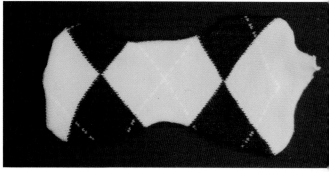

13. Gently stuff the spee-EYE-der with polyfill. Hand sew the small opening closed with matching thread. Good luck with *that* if you're using an NDGA (nuclear Day-Glo anklet) like me. Who has thread that matches that? Well, do your best.

14. Flip Ms. Spider over on her tummy. Now we're going to add those legs, and you'll see some spee-EYE-der magic when I transform 4 long legs into 8 less-long-but-equally-menacing legs. Evenly space them out on her tum, pin them in place, and stitch the middle of each leg to her tum. Hide your stitches as best you can.

15. Now let's talk eyes. Most spee-EYE-ders have 8 eyes. You may have to get creative about finding 4 sets of something to meet this requirement. I went the bling route.

16. Once you have all Ms. Spider's eyes either stitched or glued on, bend her legs into position. Now she is ready to stalk and pounce on her prey, wrap it up with silk, and devour it.

Spee-EYE-der Antics

Something wicked this way comes.

Who you calling "itsy bitsy"? Do I look itsy bitsy to you?

Well, it *might* be too much bling, but a girl's gotta have a *little* sparkle.

I have you now, my pretty!

things that want you to
stay away

Designed and made by Brenna Maloney

dastardly devilfish

Finished size: Wingspan of about 11″ (28 cm)

These sock versions of manta rays may look innocent, but remember—they don't call manta rays "devilfish" for nothing! Well … actually … full disclosure: They *do* call them devilfish for nothing. Sure, sure, long ago fishermen used to get spooked by them because some of them are ginormous. And because they can do startling things like leap out of the water and slap the surface with their wings—hard enough to capsize Mr. Fisherman's little dinghy. You know, stuff like that. But manta rays are incredibly peaceful animals. There's nothing devilish about them. They certainly have no interest in deviling the likes of *you*. In fact, they are more apt to turn tail and flee than to spend time in the company of humans. Still. You *might* be able to make yours look scary. If you try really hard.

1. Look for a sock with a contrasting heel for this pattern. I've used a single crew sock here—nothing too fancy.

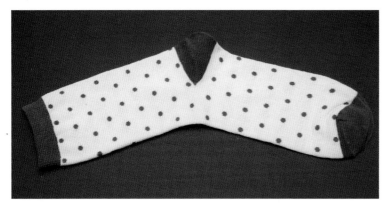

2. Fold your sock in half at the heel.

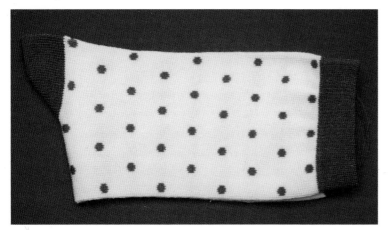

3. Using the Dastardly Devilfish pattern (page 140) or making it up as you go along, trace the shape on the sock with a marking pen and cut it out.

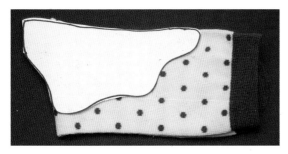

4. Unfold it. It will look something like this.

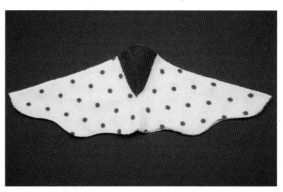

5. Now, search your lair for a bit of quilt batting to stuff the ol' girl. If we use polyfill, she'll bloat up too much, and you know no one cares for bloat. Well, maybe for sea creatures bloat is good for buoyancy, but still … it's unattractive. We'll keep her girlish figure and make her flat instead.

6. Cut 2 pieces of batting. So, if you're doing this right so far, she'll have a top and bottom, and 2 layers of innards. You'll also need to find a bit of ribbon for her tail.

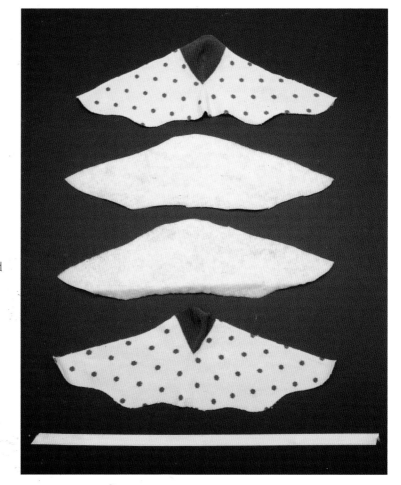

7. Before we stitch all this together, we'll want to sew a little test strip. Find a sock scrap to practice on. What we want to use is a zigzag stitch, but you might have to play with how long and how tight your stitches are. We want a pretty thick line. Thread color is up to you. You may want your stitches to stand out, or you may want them to blend in. Your choice. Note: If you want to hand stitch, try using a tight blanket stitch where I am using the zigzag.

8. Arrange the layers: belly piece facedown, 2 layers of batting, top layer faceup. Insert an end of the ribbon in Ms. Devilfish's back end. Slowly zigzag all around her perimeter.

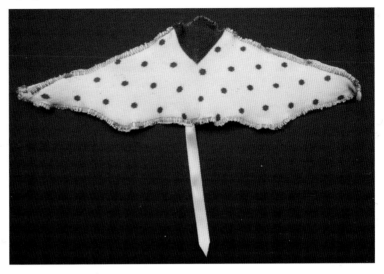

9. Using the zigzag is fun because it creates a wavy look for her body and fins.

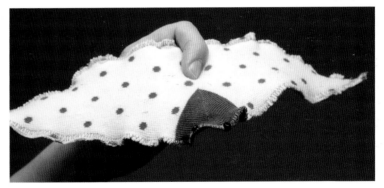

10. Add some eyes. Black seed beads make good eyes.

From the Depths

Where did everybody go?

Nice current today!

Do we look scarier like this?

Designed and made by Brenna Maloney

shifty chameleons

Finished size: About 9″ (23 cm) long, with tail coiled

Ahhhh … the shifty chameleon. Word to the wise: You cannot trust an animal whose eyes move independently of one another and who can change its color at will. Cool thing about chameleons: Most people think they change their color to camouflage themselves. In fact, chameleons change color to express emotion—to show anger or fear. Pretty interesting, huh? Yeah, until you try living with a chameleon. Then you're always guessing: Is she sad? Is she mad? If her skin turns blue and starts to flake off, should I be concerned? If she turns purple, is she just messing with me? And the thing is: You'll never know. It's not like she's going to tell you what it all means. Nooooo. She'll flame up crimson, throw that tongue out and gobble some passing insect, and then give you the eyes (one looking right at you and the other looking somewhere in the region of your left kneecap), and you'll always be wondering … what the heck did that mean?

1. Find a nice long pair of crazy, colorful knee-highs. (If you want to add a long tongue, you'll also need a longish scrap of red sock.)

2. Cut the foot sections off both socks, and then cut off the cuffs plus about 3″ (7.5 cm).

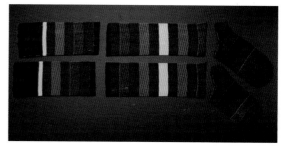

3. Cut open one side on each of the 2 middle sections.

4. Open and lay them flat.

5. Copy the Shifty Chameleons body pattern (page 141) and trace it onto the back side of a section. Then, place that section on top of the other section with right sides together. Sew sloooowly, especially around Ms. Chameleon's tail. And remember to leave a little gap open on her tum so we can turn her..

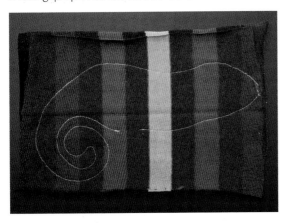

6. Trim away the excess sockage, then cut her head off. Don't be so squeamish. It's only temporary, you big baby. We're going to put it back on in a second!

7. Set the Headless Wonder aside and go back to one of your cuffed pieces. Lop off the cuff.

8. Turn the cuff inside out and sew a large U from one end to the other. This is going to be the chameleon's "thing." You know, that part that they have on their necks.

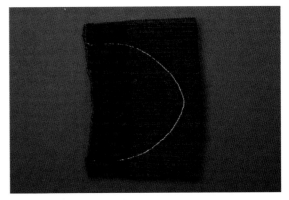

9. Trim away the excess sockage, and turn.

10. Good, good. We're going to insert it in her neck and sew her noggin back on. See? I told you the whole head-neck separation was only temporary.

11. Wiggle the "thing" into place.

12. You might want to pin it to keep things from sliding around as you line up the head, "thing," and neck.

13. Slowly stitch everything in place.

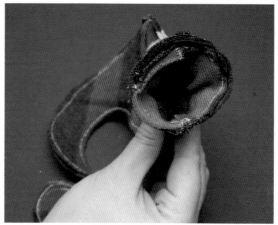

14. Now, when you start to turn Ms. Chameleon, you can see how the "thing" works into the equation.

15. Do you remember that nifty hemostat doo-hickey I told you about in Pokers (page 6)? Now is a good time to check your tool belt for that thing, because turning her tail is a bit of a nightmare. Take a deep breath. Just go slow. Turn the tail.

16. The tail might start to spiral a bit as you go. That's okay—just try not to yank on it too much. No animal likes having its tail yanked. Didn't your mother teach you anything?

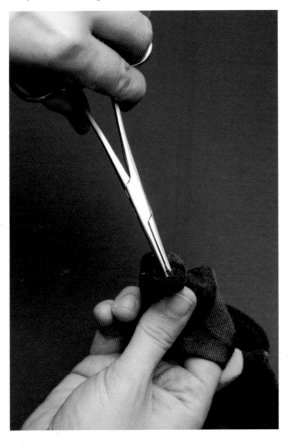

Here's how things look when laid flat after turning.

17. Now let's get to work on the arms and legs. Turn your 2 leftover sock-cuff segments inside out. You can use the Shifty Chameleons arm and leg patterns (page 141), or you can free sew the shapes. We need 2 legs and 2 arms, with 2 toes/fingers on each. Be sure to leave a small gap on each as you stitch, so you can turn them.

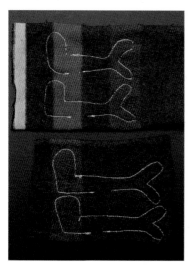

18. Cut out and turn the limbs. You'll probably need your hemostat thing again. Ms. Chameleon is going to need a lot of upper-body strength, so add support with pipe cleaners. Create little arm and leg scaffolds, with loops for the toes and fingers. Once you insert them into a limb, hand stitch the gap closed. Do this for all 4 limbs. Don't hurry. It's okay. I'll wait. I'll do a little light reading: "Understanding Your Chameleon: A Mother's Trip to Madness."

19. We're going to begin to stuff her with polyfill now, but we aren't going to get very far before I ask you to do something weird. Stuff the top portion of her head close to the nose. Then flatten that part out with your fingers.

20. Chameleons have neat little lips (well, I guess they are lips) that we are going to create by stitching a line across the bridge of her nose. You can do this by hand, although I just zipped mine across on my sewing machine. It doesn't have to be perfect ... or, looking at mine here, I see it doesn't even have to be particularly straight. (Hmmm ... no, I was not drinking while working on this project but you may well wonder ...) Well, it doesn't bother me when things look wonky. I'm sure you will take more care with yours.

21. Finish stuffing her. It's up to you, but you might want to add a pipe cleaner in her tail, just to help keep its shape. I didn't stuff her tail much; I started the heavy stuffing at the base of her butt and worked my way back up to the head. Make sure to stitch closed the gap we left in her tum.

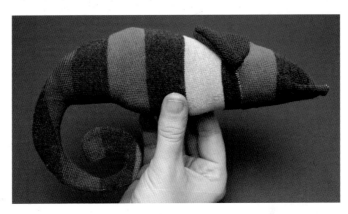

22. Using a matching thread (or anything close to it), hand stitch her arms and legs on.

23. The eyes really make this pattern. Chameleons have such funky, funky eyes. Think about stacking beads and making her eyes really tall. Try sewing them on unevenly, so one is higher than the other. She's all set.

tip

If you want to add a tongue, it's easy enough to do. Make a long tube from a red sock, just wide enough to slip a pipe cleaner into. Turn the tube and insert the pipe cleaner. Turn the raw edges under and hand stitch the tube onto the bottom of the chameleon's mouth. Then you can bend her tongue in whatever position you want to.

◇ **Technicolor Chameleon** ◇

If you want to have a little fun, try adding some texture to
your chameleon. If you look at a real chameleon up close,
you'll see its skin is covered in tiny bumps. To try to create
that look, I made an all-white chameleon. Then I took a
foam brush and slathered on iridescent paint. (I used
Jacquard Lumiere acrylic paint.) On her head, I sprinkled
tiny glass beads over the wet paint. I warn you: Those little
glass balls go skittering everywhere, but it does create a neat
effect. She'll need a couple of days to dry before you can
safely add eyes. When she's all finished, she really sparkles!

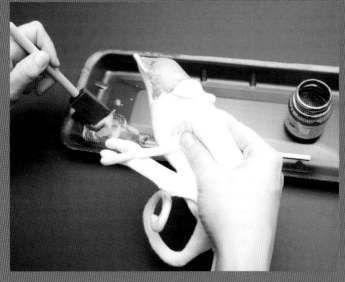

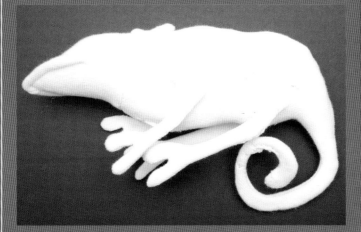

Masters of Mood

Uh ... I believe I have the right of way.

"Do you want to talk about your feelings?"
"No."
"Really? Because maybe we should talk about our feelings."

Closer ... closer ... closer ...

Needs catsup.

Designed and made by Brenna Maloney

tricky armadillos

Finished size: About 10″ (25.5 cm) long (uncurled!)

Interesting beasts, armadillos. The Aztec called them *azotochtli*, meaning "turtle-rabbit." That hurts my brain to think about, crossing a turtle and a rabbit, but there you have it. Armadillos are survivors. And they can be tricky. When the going gets tough, some of them can curl up into an armored ball. Predators—Aztec, perhaps?—can kick them around, but they can't get in. I've used this same strategy at work when my boss comes looking for me. Sadly, though, my "tough-guy armadillo" stance is usually mistaken for "defeated fetal ball" mode. I'll have to work on that. But armadillos, man, they've got it going on.

1. Find the longest sock you can. I mean really, really, really long.

2. Cut off the foot section and the cuff. Cut the long section in half.

3. Cut one of the long section halves down both sides so you have 2 matching pieces. Put them aside for a moment.

4. Slice the other segment into 5 even pieces. Why are you doing this? All will be revealed in good time, my friend. You are creating the armor for your little armadillo right now.

5. Take each of these newly sliced little tubes and cut the sides to make 2 matching pieces—a total of 10 pieces. Are you exhausted yet? Yeah, this is time consuming, I'm afraid, but the effect will be very cool and worth it. It will be "socktacular," as my children now like to say. (Do you think they are mocking me?)

6. Now fold each of these little slices in half lengthwise.

7. Go back to one of the long sections you cut in Step 3. Lay a folded slice at the very end of this piece, with the fold facing off the end of the sock strip. Sew this piece in place. Use matching thread—not white thread as I am doing for demonstration purposes.

8. Repeat Step 7, laying another folded strip on top of the strip you just sewed down.

9. Repeat until you've sewn all 10 strips in place.

10. Pick this piece up, and you'll see how it can accordion. You can also see why you need to use a matching thread!

11. The next 2 steps will have you swearing I'm crazy. I am. A little. But I want to hide a seam, so you'll understand what I'm doing in a minute. Go to the seam of the last folded strip and slice off the extra sockage.

12. Now sew it back on. Yeah, I know: stupid. But what it does is attach Armadillo's head to her body with no ugly seam on top. Some reader in Canada will likely devise a better way, and I'll share it with you then.

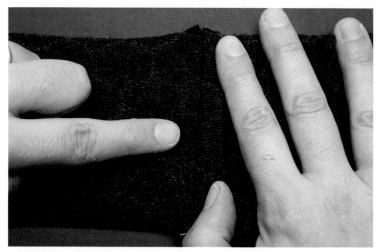

13. Now. Lay the whole piece flat on a cutting mat or a piece of heavy cardboard. Very close to the seam you just sewed, use your rotary cutter to slice 2 little slits where we will insert ears. It looks like I am cutting off one of my fingers here. I'm not. I just love doing this to vex my publisher. I think my publisher always worries a little that I might lead you astray. Obviously, do *not* cut off any fingers while you are doing this. (By the way, you'll also notice that I'm left-handed.)

14. Here you can see that my 2 fingers are quite safe, poking through to where we will insert ears.

15. Did I mention ears? Well, what the heck?! I haven't had you sew any ears. What kind of lame operation *is* this anyway? No worries, my friend. Turn your sock's foot section inside out and free sew a pair of ears. While you're at it, trace the Tricky Armadillos legs and arms patterns (page 142) and sew a pair of each. Don't forget to leave gaps for turning.

16. Trim away the excess sockage. She's saying, "Hallelujah!" and kicking up her heels here.

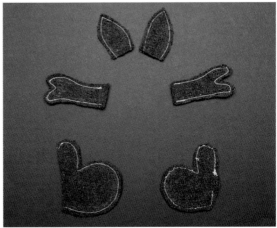

17. Turn the ears, and insert them in the holes on your armadillo's head. You can hand stitch them in place or use your machine very slooooooowly. Here's how it looks when you lay everything flat.

18. Place the remaining piece of sock you cut out in Step 3 on top of the accordion piece, right sides together. Now sew an armadillo shape! *Do what?* Well, think of it as sort of a skinny, pointed oval. Leave a midsize gap for turning. Turn!

19. Lightly stuff Armadillo's body, and hand stitch the gap closed with matching thread. Don't overstuff her; you want to be able to roll her up.

20. Please give her some beady little eyes. Now, sew half of a tiny snap to the underside of her nose, and the other half onto her back, in the first or second band.

21. We're getting close, but we still have some limbs to consider. Turn those and lightly stuff them. Hand stitch the gaps closed with matching thread.

22. Take a break. Eat a few Junior Mints or candy of your choice. You've been putting forth an incredible amount of effort here.

23. We want to be able to move Armadillo's limbs, so sew some little buttons on her arms and legs. You are ready to move on when all 4 limbs look like this.

Here's how she looks with all limbs in place.

She's ready to roll at the slightest provocation, so watch what you say to her!

24. To attach her legs, run a long tapestry needle through the button and the leg, through her body, and out the other side through the opposite leg and button. Sew through each leg several times, being careful not to cinch things too tightly. Her back legs should not sink into her body; they should just be firmly attached. Repeat this process for her arms.

On a Roll

A rolling stone gathers no moss.

And now for our next amazing trick ... !

I can't quite reach ... a little higher, please.

things you can't avoid

avoid

Designed and made by Brenna Maloney

sticky-fingered gremlins

Finished size: About 9″ (23 cm) tall

These guys. Yeah. *These* are the guys responsible every time your car keys go missing. Or you can't find the remote. Or your other earring. Or your cell phone … They're Sticky-Fingered Gremlins, aren't they? They love messing with your day by making those things that you can't function without go missing.

1. Since they are quite the tricksters, you're going to want to look for a really wild sock to make a Gremlin. Look for a knee-high to give you plenty of room to work.

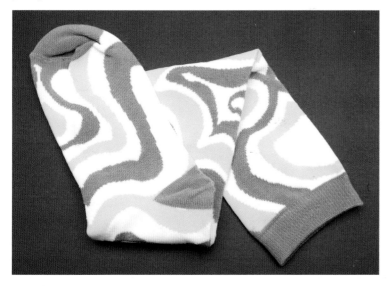

2. Turn your knee-high inside out. Cut off the cuff with about 4" (10 cm) of sock. We'll save that part for later.

3. You're going to unleash your inner demon here and go wild with the free sewing. Gremlins have funky little heads. Fold the heel down on your sock to get it out of the way. Above the heel, free sew several spikies with blobs on the end. There's no right or wrong way to do it. Make them as uneven and as tall as you like. The more lopsided, the better. Truth be told, Gremlins are so busy messing with your day, they often take little pride in their own personal appearance. I believe they also smell. Pretty badly.

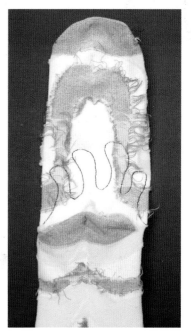

4. Once you've got some funkiness going on up top, cut off the toe section of the sock above your stitched lines. Keep that piece for later, though. Now let's give the dude some little legs—so he can scamper out of sight with your car keys as you come around the corner looking for them. I stitched a simple U at the cut-off end of the sock (opposite the head end). Leave his toes open so you can turn him.

5. With the toe section of the sock inside out, free sew 2 arms, about 1½" (4 cm) long. That will give him a good long reach when he's stealing that last donut. I've given mine 3 fingers on each hand. (*Optional:* If you want to give him an almighty grip, insert a little pipe cleaner scaffolding into his fingers, hands, and arms.)

6. Trim away the excess sockage and give him a turn.

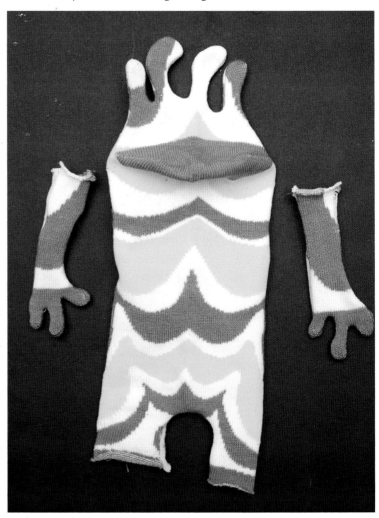

7. Stuff him with polyfill. Don't stuff his spikies, just his head. Seal up his toesies by using a running stitch (like gathering). Pull each toe shut and knot the thread firmly.

8. Tuck the raw edges of his arms under at the shoulder and sew the arms onto the sides of the body.

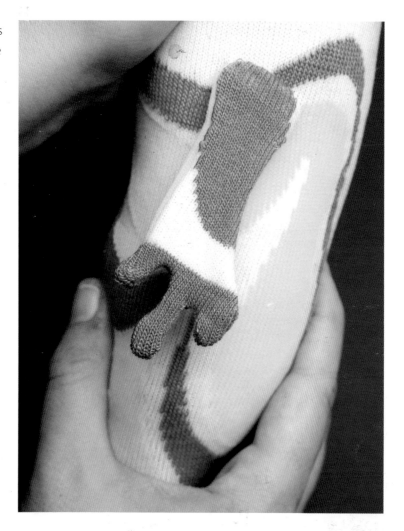

9. Give him a sly smile. I made mine sort of curvy with a few strands of black embroidery floss.

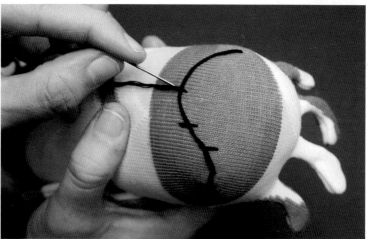

10. Gremlins always have their eyes open for things with the maximum pain factor for you—the thing that will cause the longest delay, or the thing that will have you openly weeping because you can't find it and have convinced yourself that your powers of mental acuity are slipping away faster than you realize. So, we like to give these dudes *mega-swirly* eyes. (Yes, that is the technical term I'm using there.) Here's how: Look through your pile of felt (because I *know* you have one. Who doesn't have a pile of felt in their lair?) and find 2 really strong colors. Cut a thin strip from each.

11. Stack the strips and slowly roll them up. How big should you make it? Dime-size or so, I'd guess. It's up to you, really.

12. With a needle and matching thread, tack the end of the swirl. Trim off the excess. Make 2.

13. I tacked mine onto his head with a hot glue gun. Mostly because it was easy and because I just love scorching my fingers, which I seem to do virtually every time I use that thing. You can save yourself the burn, though, and just stitch them in place. Now the Gremlin is all set to hide your valuables from you!

You can experiment with button or bead eyes, or change floss colors for a different look for his mouth.

Gremlins in Action

Let's start by taking your car keys ...

Cell phone? Mine!

The remote! Ha! They won't be able to function without *this*!

Now we'll orphan a sock!

Designed and made by Brenna Maloney

bad guys

About 14" (35.5 cm) tall

Do you want to play cops and robbers? How about just robber? Robber is bound to be more fun! Let's see now … who do we want to rob? The Junior Mint factory? Tempting, tempting. My bank? Even more tempting. … Ah, but there's always the prospect of getting caught. And then, you know, there's prison. And horizontal stripes make me look fat. Well, *fatter*, anyway. We all know crime doesn't pay, and most criminals aren't the brightest bulbs. That's also true in the sock world. These sock bad guys are like the Keystone Kops of crime. They're idiots. They're numbskulls. They're boobs. And they're really fun to make.

1. We're going to need a lot of sockage to pull off this project. At least a black knee-high (the ribbed cuff should be at least 2″ [5 cm] long), a white anklet (or piece of white sock you have lying around), and something in black and white stripes. I had a pair of striped anklets. Find whatever you have.

2. Let's do a little snip, snip, snipping. Cut the foot section off your black knee-high. Also cut off the ribbed cuff (plus a few inches). Cut a 3″ (7.5 cm) segment of stripes for Mr. Bad Guy's arms, and a 1½″ (4 cm) segment of white for his hannies (Brennaspeak translation: *hands*). You'll also need a 2″ (5 cm) segment of white for his head, and a 2½″ (6.5 cm) striped segment for his chest.

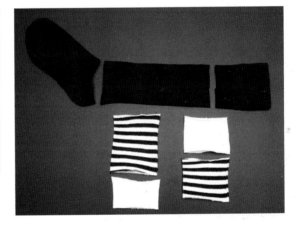

3. We'll get his body under way first. Take the head, chest, and leg pieces, and slice them open along one side.

4. Open them flat and sew them together. Set this aside.

5. Cut the striped and white arm and hannies pieces open along one side. Stitch the sections together.

6. Free sew 2 arm/hannie combos. I shaped his hands almost as if they were wearing mittens. Why would a robber wear mittens? I don't know. Like I said earlier, most criminals aren't very bright. Maybe this one had cold hannies.

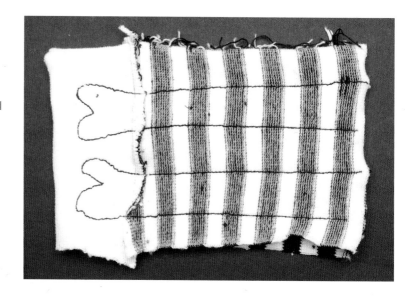

7. Trim away any excess sockage and turn these.

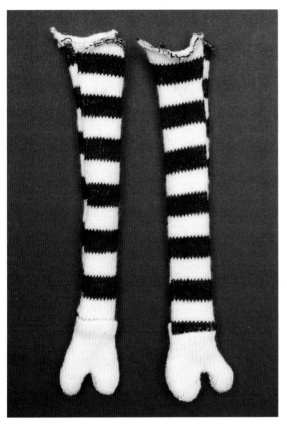

8. Go back to the body piece. Fold this in half, right sides together, with the fold on the right. We're going to sew Mr. Bad Guy's head, and sew his arms in place at the same time. Cut open the fold just along the white/striped portion so you can slip the right arm in. Insert both arms between the front and back body, with the hands facing inward; pin.

9. Start at his waist and sew upward. Round his shoulders and free sew his round little head. Finish the other shoulder and stop at the waist.

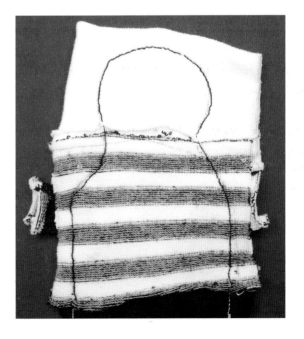

10. I've switched thread so you can see this next part. On the bottom, black section, we're going to free sew his butt and 2 skinny, skinny legs. Leave a small gap in one of his sides so we can turn him.

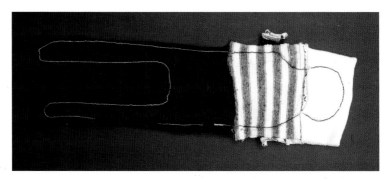

11. Give him a turn. He's got open arms for you! (Watch your pockets if he hugs you, though. Just saying.)

12. Let's work on a little pipe cleaner scaffolding for his legs.

13. Carefully insert the scaffolding into his legs. Lightly stuff his head, chest, tum, and butt with polyfill. Sew up the gap we left for turning.

14. He'll need a Bad Guy thug cap, so go back to what's left of your black sock. We only want the ribbed cuff. Turn it inside out and sew a large U.

15. Turn it, and you'll see we have a little thug cap!

16. Bad Guy needs a Bad Guy Mask, which we can cut out of black felt. Cut out a figure 8 and then cut eye holes. Hand stitch the mask onto his face with black thread. Add black seed beads for eyes.

17. Stitch on a lopsided grin with a few strands of black embroidery floss. (He's bad, but he's not *all* bad.) Put on his thug cap, and he's ready to break into your home!

Mug Shots

Smile for the birdie, boys. You're going away for a long time.

What!? It's the only clean shirt I had!

Take the money and run.

Mine! All mine!

Dude. Crime does not pay.

Designed and made by Brenna Maloney

dastardly devils

Finished size: About 7½" (19 cm) tall, from hoof to horns

He's *the Devil*. You know, Satan. Lucifer. Beelzebub. The Prince of Darkness. The Son of Perdition. Mephistopheles. No matter what you call him, he's bad news. And he's made out of a *sock*. Although, admittedly, when I look at him, he doesn't seem very sinister. He looks, well, a little goofy. I think he might be a bumbler. A not-so-nefarious devil. He doesn't really *look* capable of stealing your soul. But that could also be the way he tricks people. …

1. We'll start with a nice red knee-high and a black crew sock.

2. You'll need to cut these socks into a number of segments. Cut a 5″ (12.5 cm) piece of red for our devil's body and a 1″ (2.5 cm) piece of black for his hooves. For his arms, cut a 3″ (7.5 cm) section of red and a 1″ (2.5 cm) section of black for his … uh … what do you call his "hands"? Hooves there, too, I guess? Also cut a 2½″ (6.5 cm) section of red for his face, a 1″ (2.5 cm) section of black for his horns, and a ¾″ (2 cm) section of black for his beard. You got all those? And could I please also have fries with that?

3. Let's start with his lower half. Cut the red body piece and the black hoof piece open along one side.

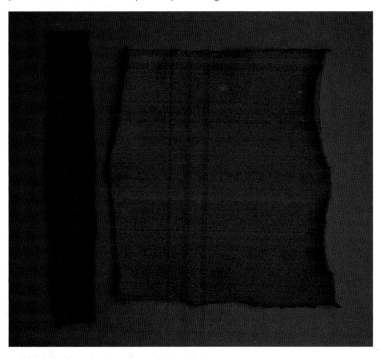

4. Sew these 2 pieces together, please.

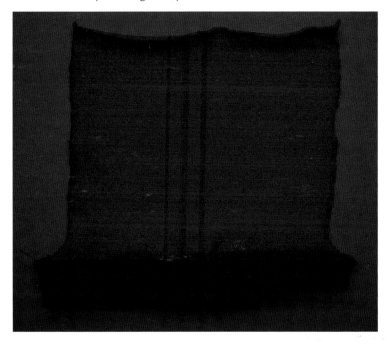

5. Now fold this section in half, with right sides together. This piece will become the devil's lower body and his tail, which you'll free sew as 2 separate pieces. The body is a long, skinny tube until you get down to the last quarter of the section, where you'll create 2 legs. Each leg should have a 2-toed black hoof at the end. It's a little hard to see here, so we've drawn some lines on top of the photo to help guide you. The tail is a long, thin red tube with a black arrow at the bottom.

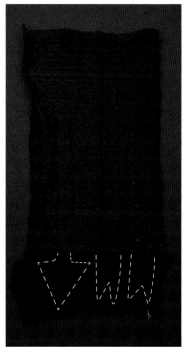

6. Once we trim away the extra sockage, you can see things a bit more clearly. You can go ahead and turn him now.

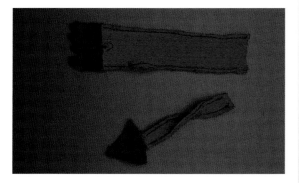

7. Put the evil little husk aside for a moment, and let's return to the arm pieces—the 3″ (7.5 cm) piece of red and the 1″ (2.5 cm) piece of black. Cut these tubes open along one side and stitch the 2 pieces together.

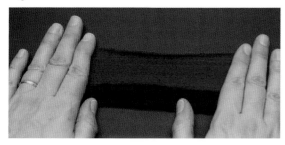

8. Fold this piece in half with right sides together. Free sew 2 red arms with 2-fingered black hooves on each.

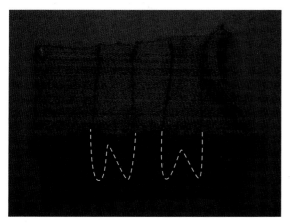

9. Trim away the excess sockage and gently turn.

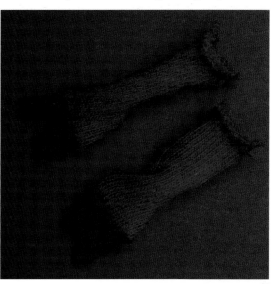

10. Go back to your remaining pieces for the head, horns, and beard. Stop me if you've heard this one before, but … cut these pieces open along one side and stitch them together. The red piece should be in the middle and the slightly wider black piece on top.

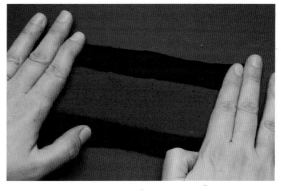

11. Fold this piece in half with right sides together. Here we'll sew a triangular head with 2 slightly curved horns in black. On the bottom is a pointy black beard. Leave a small opening on the devil's cheek so we can turn him.

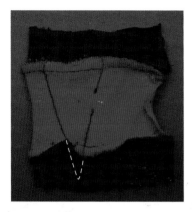

12. Trim away the excess you-know-what, and turn.

13. We can do a little bit of wiring, if you like, to give Mr. Devil some flexibility. Start by inserting a pipe cleaner into his tail.

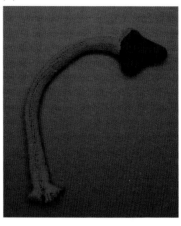

14. Next, bend a pipe cleaner to make 2 legs, make 2 little loops for "toes" on each leg, and insert into his lower body.

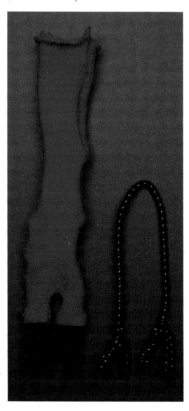

15. While you're at it, you can stuff a little polyfill in his chest and tum.

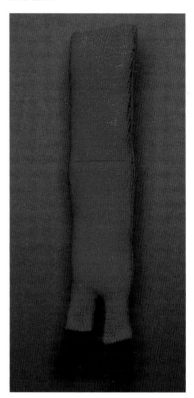

16. Seal off his neck by tucking the raw edges under and using a slip stitch across the opening.

17. Stuff his head with a little polyfill, and now let's work on his face. Black eyes, of course. See how they smolder? And let's give him what my oldest son always calls "mad eyes." That means add some angry eyebrows stitched with a few strands of black embroidery floss.

19. You can attach the 'stache with needle and thread or a spot of hot glue—your choice. And stitch him a little angry mouth. This devil means business.

20. Stitch his head onto his shoulders. Where you position the head relative to the chest is your call. I put the end of the beard nearly 2" (5 cm) down. Try different positions; see which one looks the most absurd, and stick with that.

21. Add his arms next; turn the raw edges inside and stitch them to the shoulders. You can slip a piece of pipe cleaner into each arm first if you want to give him flexibility there, too.

22. Tack on that tail in the back and he's ready for soul stealing!

18. Now find a small piece of black felt and cut out a little handlebar mustache. Do devils have handlebar mustaches? I don't know. I think they must, though. To go with their little goatee beards.

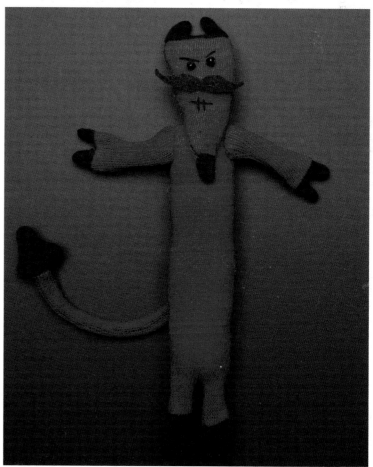

Den o' Devils

It *is* hot down there. But it's a *dry heat*.

We've been waiting for you, my friend!

You did *not* just ask me for a glass of water!

Is that the cry of someone who has eaten her *last* Junior Mint?

patterns

Snowman Assassins *Body*

(project on page 14)

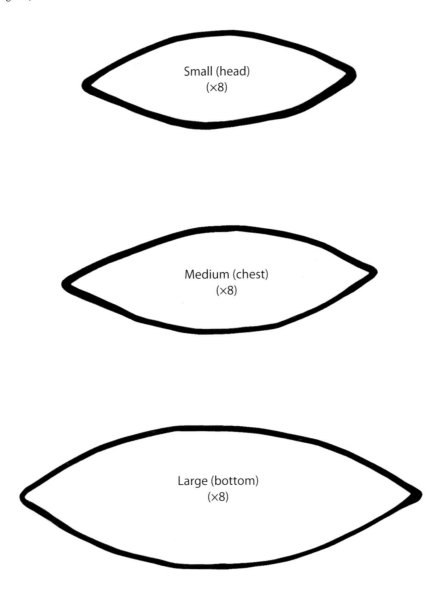

Small (head)
(×8)

Medium (chest)
(×8)

Large (bottom)
(×8)

Snowman Assassins *Hat*

(project on page 14)

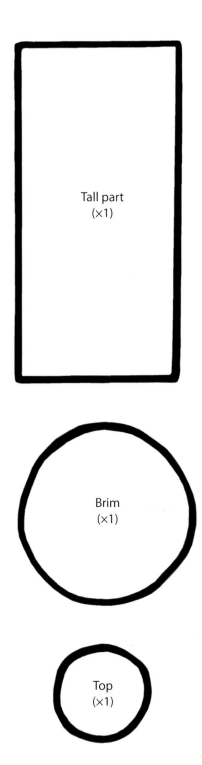

Tall part
(×1)

Brim
(×1)

Top
(×1)

Evil Clowns

(project on page 22)

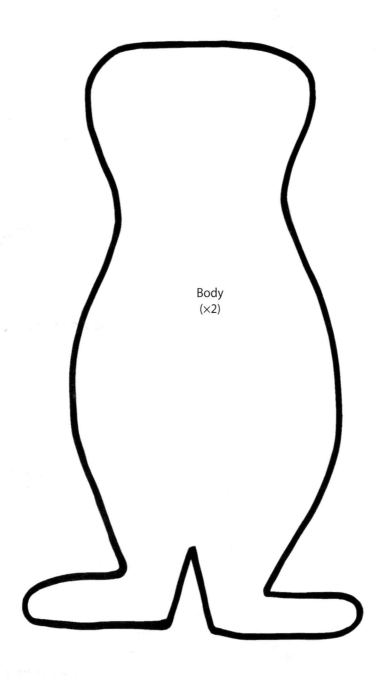

Body
(×2)

Sinister Anglerfish

(project on page 28)

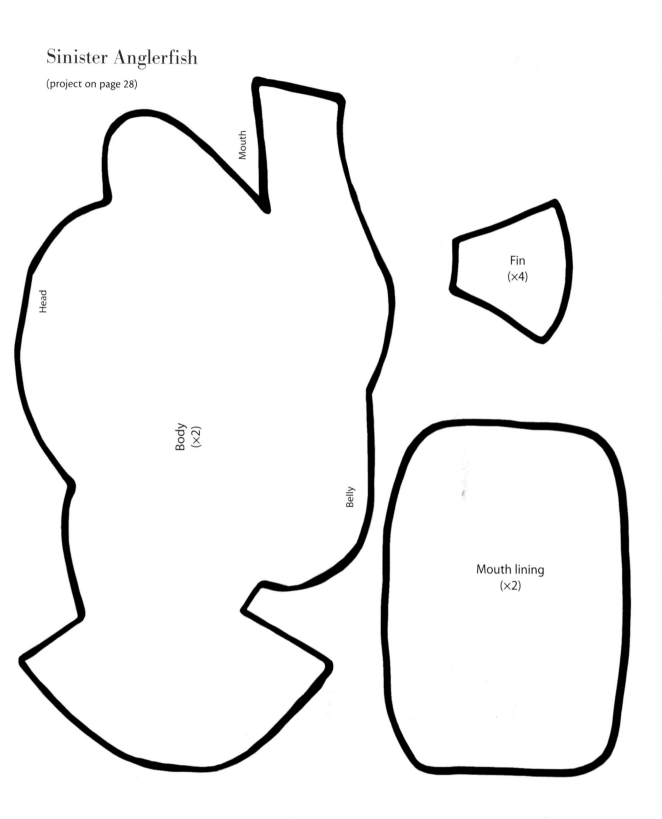

Mouth

Head

Body
(×2)

Belly

Fin
(×4)

Mouth lining
(×2)

Blood-Sucking Bats

(project on page 38)

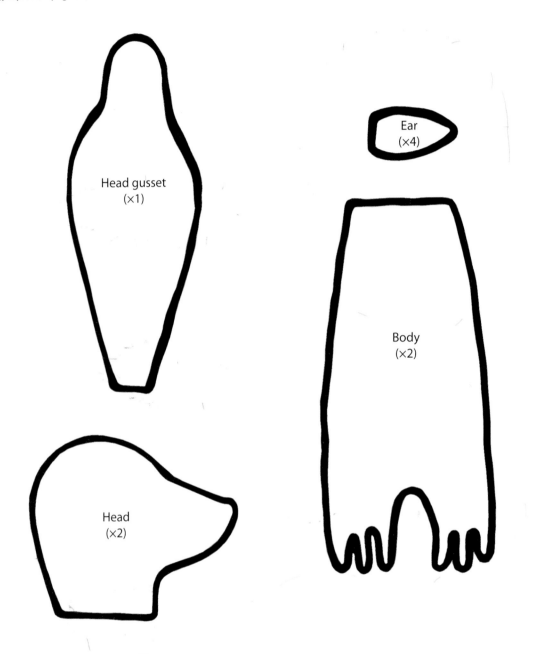

Ear
(×4)

Head gusset
(×1)

Body
(×2)

Head
(×2)

Wicked Weeds

(project on page 60)

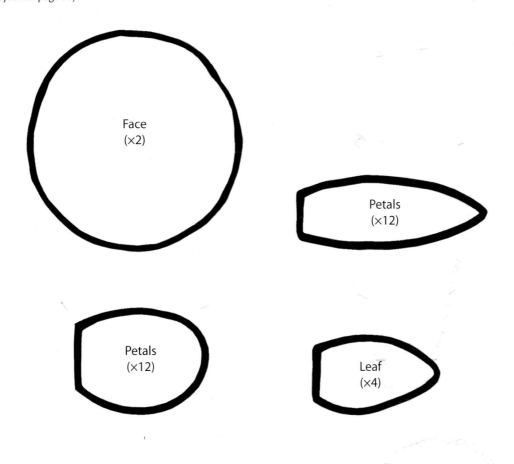

Face
(×2)

Petals
(×12)

Petals
(×12)

Leaf
(×4)

Evil Evil Bad Yucky Grasshopper

(project on page 74)

Body
(×4)

Evil head
(×2)

Not-So-Itsy-Bitsy Spiders

(project on page 80)

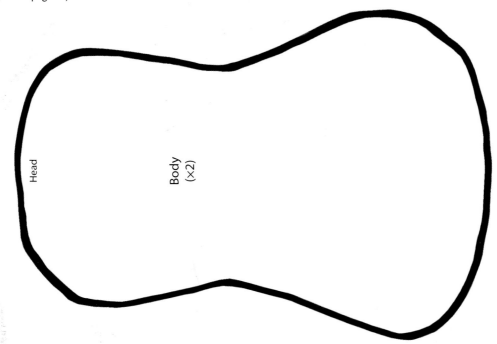

Head

Body
(×2)

Dastardly Devilfish

(project on page 88)

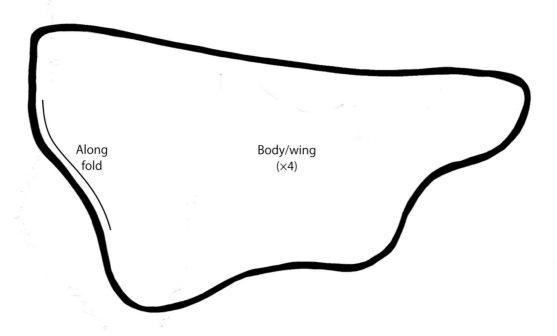

Along
fold

Body/wing
(×4)

Shifty Chameleons

(project on page 94)

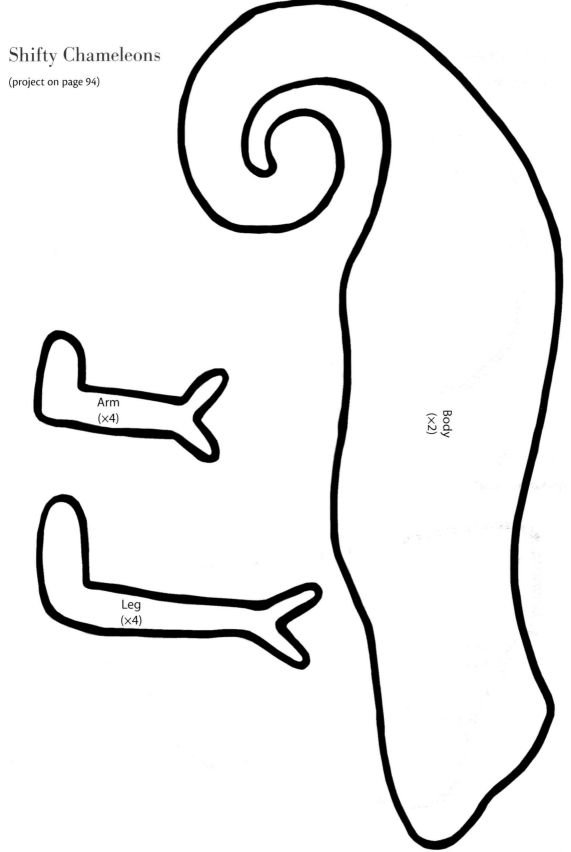

Arm
(×4)

Leg
(×4)

Body
(×2)

Tricky Armadillos

(project on page 104)

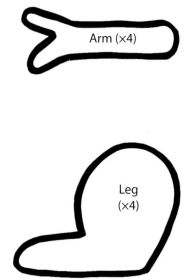

Arm (×4)

Leg
(×4)

final thoughts

Well, they say there is a very fine line between "hobby" and "mental illness." I'm not sure if we've crossed that line or not. I may very well have, but you're probably still okay. I promised my publisher that if they would publish this third book about socks, I would stop it and go seek help. Guess I need to make good on that promise. (Although … I never signed anything official on that, did I?) A friend suggested I try making things out of underwear, but that's probably too weird, right? Maybe I'll just stick to socks.

Guess I'll head back down to the lair now. … I did have a few new ideas, even though I tried not to. If you need anything, you let me know. I'm easy to find.

Until next time,

—Brenna

about the author

Brenna Maloney is the author of *Socks Appeal* and *Sockology*. She lives with her husband and sons in Washington, D.C.

Follow Brenna on her blog at brennamaloney.com.

Also by Brenna Maloney:

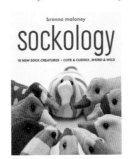

Also available as an eBook

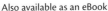